TWELFTH NIGHT

WILLIAM SHAKESPEARE

NOTES BY DAVID PINNINGTON

Longman

YORK PRESS
322 Old Brompton Road, London SW5 9JH

PEARSON EDUCATION LIMITED
Edinburgh Gate, Harlow,
Essex CM20 2JE, United Kingdom
Associated companies, branches and representatives throughout the world

First published 1997
This new and fully revised edition first published 2002
Fourth impression 2006

10 9 8 7 6 5 4

ISBN-10: 0-582-50629-8
ISBN-13: 978-0-582-50629-9

Designed by Michelle Cannatella
Illustrated by Tony Chance
Phototypeset by Gem Graphics, Trenance, Mawgan Porth, Cornwall
Colour reproduction and film output by Spectrum Colour
Produced by Pearson Education Asia Limited, Hong Kong

PREFACE

York Notes are designed to give you a broader perspective on works of literature studied at GCSE and equivalent levels. With examination requirements changing in the twenty-first century, we have made a number of significant changes to this new series. We continue to help students to reach their own interpretations of the text but York Notes now have important extra-value new features.

You will discover that York Notes are genuinely interactive. The new **Checkpoint** features make sure that you can test your knowledge and broaden your understanding. You will also be directed to excellent websites, books and films where you can follow up ideas for yourself.

The **Resources** section has been updated and an entirely new section has been devoted to how to improve your grade. Careful reading and application of the principles laid out in the Resources section guarantee improved performance.

The **Detailed summaries** include an easy-to-follow skeleton structure of the story-line, while the section on **Language and style** has been extended to offer an in-depth discussion of the writer's techniques.

The Contents page shows the structure of this study guide. However, there is no need to read from the beginning to the end as you would with a novel, play or poem. Use the Notes in the way that suits you. Our aim is to help you with your understanding of the work, not to dictate how you should learn.

Our authors are practising English teachers and examiners who have used their experience to offer a whole range of **Examiner's secrets** – useful hints to encourage exam success.

The General Editor of this series is John Polley, Senior GCSE Examiner and former Head of English at Harrow Way Community School, Andover.

The author of these Notes is David Pinnington. David read English at the universities of York and Exeter, where he took an MA in Modern Fiction. He teaches in Devon and is a Senior GCSE Examiner for English and English Literature.

The text used in these Notes is the Arden Shakespeare Series, Routledge, 1975.

Part One

Introduction

How to study a play

Though it may seem obvious, remember that a play is written to be performed before an audience. Ideally, you should see the play live on stage. A film or video recording is next best, though neither can capture the enjoyment of being in a theatre and realising that your reactions are part of the performance.

There are six aspects of a play:

1. THE PLOT: a play is a story whose events are carefully organised by the playwright in order to show how a situation can be worked out
2. THE CHARACTERS: these are the people who have to face this situation. Since they are human they can be good or bad, clever or stupid, likeable or detestable, etc. They may change too!
3. THE THEMES: these are the underlying messages of the play, e.g. jealousy can cause the worst of crimes; ambition can bring the mightiest low
4. THE SETTING: this concerns the time and place that the author has chosen for the play
5. THE LANGUAGE: the writer uses a certain style of expression to convey the characters and ideas
6. STAGING AND PERFORMANCE: the type of stage, the lighting, the sound effects, the costumes, the acting styles and delivery must all be decided

Work out the choices the dramatist has made in the first four areas, and consider how a director might balance these choices to create a live performance.

The purpose of these York Notes is to help you understand what the play is about and to enable you to make your own interpretation. Do not expect the study of a play to be neat and easy: plays are chosen for examination purposes, not written for them!

EXAMINER'S SECRET

In your essays include reference to some aspect of stagecraft for a particular scene or speech.

AUTHOR – LIFE AND WORKS

1564 William Shakespeare is baptised on 26 April in Stratford-on-Avon, Warwickshire

1582 Marries Anne Hathaway

1583 Birth of daughter, Susanna

1585 Birth of twins, Hamnet and Judith

1590–93 Early published works and poems written when theatres are closed by the Plague

1594 Joins Lord Chamberlain's Men (from 1603 named the King's Men) as actor and playwright

1595 *Romeo and Juliet* first performed

1595–9 Writes the history plays and comedies

1597 Shakespeare buys New Place, the second biggest house in Stratford

1599 Moves to newly-opened Globe Theatre

1599–1608 Writes his greatest plays, including *Macbeth*, *King Lear* and *Hamlet*

1600–01 Writes *Twelfth Night*

1608–13 Takes over the lease of Blackfriars Theatre and writes final plays, the romances, ending with *The Tempest*

1609 Shakespeare's sonnets published

1613 Globe Theatre burns down 29 June, during performance of *Henry VIII*

1616 Shakespeare dies, 23 April, and is buried in Stratford

1623 First Folio of Shakespeare's plays published

CONTEXT

1558 Elizabeth I becomes Queen of England

1568 Mary Queen of Scots is imprisoned for life

1577–88 Sir Francis Drake becomes the first to circumnavigate the world

1587 Mary Queen of Scots is executed

1588 Defeat of the Spanish Armada

1591 Tea is first drunk in England

1593–4 Outbreak of the Plague in London, closing theatres and killing as many as 5,000 people, according to some sources

1594 Queen Elizabeth spends Christmas at Greenwich and is entertained by leading theatre company of her day, headed by James Burbage, William Kempe and Shakespeare

1595 Walter Raleigh sails to Guiana

1599 Oliver Cromwell is born

1603 Elizabeth I dies on 24 March; James I, son of Mary, succeeds to throne of England

1604 Peace treaty signed with Spain

1605 The Gunpowder Plot

1611 The Bible is translated into the Authorised (King James) Version

1614 Fire sweeps through Stratford but New Place is spared

1618 Thirty Years War begins

SETTING AND BACKGROUND

SHAKESPEARE'S BACKGROUND

Family life

William Shakespeare was born at Stratford-upon-Avon in 1564. There is a record of his christening, 26 April, so we can assume he was born shortly before that date. His father, John Shakespeare, was a glove-maker and trader who later became high bailiff of Stratford; his mother, Mary Arden, was the daughter of a landowner. It is probable that William would have attended the local grammar school where the curriculum included Latin rhetoric, logic and literature.

In 1582 Shakespeare married Anne Hathaway, a woman eight years older than himself, and their first child, Susanna, was christened in May 1583. Two other children were born to Anne and William in 1585, the twins Hamnet and Judith. Both Shakespeare's daughters lived to marry and produce children, but Hamnet only lived till he was eleven – his burial took place in Stratford on 11 August 1596.

Writing

Sometime after 1585 Shakespeare left Stratford and went to London where he became an actor and a dramatist. He worked first with a group of actors called Lord Pembroke's Men and later with a company called the Lord Chamberlain's Men (later the King's Men). His earliest plays, *Henry IV Parts 1–3*, *Richard III*, *Titus Andronicus* and the comedies *The Comedy of Errors*, *The Taming of the Shrew* and *The Two Gentlemen of Verona* were performed around 1590–4. Shakespeare was very successful in the theatre from the start and his genius inspired the resentment of one man, Robert Greene, a mediocre university-educated dramatist who described him to his friends as 'an upstart Crow, beautified with our feathers'.

In the 1590s Shakespeare wrote six more comedies, culminating in *Twelfth Night* in 1601. During this time he also wrote history plays, tragedies and the narrative poems, *Venus and Adonis* and *The Rape of Lucrece*, in addition to the Sonnets which were published in 1609. In the early years of the new century he turned his attentions almost exclusively to tragedy and wrote some of the most powerful works in this **genre** that have ever existed: *Hamlet* (1604–5), *Othello* (1604–5),

DID YOU KNOW?

Twenty-four clay pipe fragments found near William Shakespeare's home in Stratford may have been used to smoke marijuana, cocaine, and other hallucinogenic substances.

CHECK THE BOOK

William Shakespeare: A Compact Documentary Life by S. Schoenbaum, (1987) is an excellent source of biographical information.

Macbeth (1605–6), *King Lear* (1606–7) and *Antony and Cleopatra* (1606–7).

Although Shakespeare lived and worked for most of his life in London, he obviously did not forget Stratford. In 1596 he acquired the right to a coat of arms there, something his father had tried and failed to do, and in 1597 he bought a large house in the town called New Place. Later, in 1602, he acquired other property, and in about 1610 he returned to live in Stratford permanently.

Play-writing occupied Shakespeare until the final years of his life and between 1608–12 he produced the so-called 'last plays', *Pericles*, *Cymbeline*, *The Winter's Tale* and *The Tempest*. These plays suggest a mellowing in outlook and a concern for the relationships of parents and children, as if they were written by a man who was taking stock of his life and thinking of the next generation.

Shakespeare wrote a will in January 1616, leaving bequests to Stratford acquaintances and to his actor-friends, Burbage, Heminges and Condell. The latter pair edited the first complete edition of Shakespeare's works, the First Folio of 1623. He died on 23 April.

CONTEXT AND SETTING

The Feast of 'Twelfth Night'

By the fifteenth century 'Twelfth Night' was banned from church by the French government due to lewd behaviour.

'Twelfth Night' was the name given to the last day of the Elizabethan Christmas celebrations, a feast day which was celebrated enthusiastically across the land. It ended a two-week series of festivities and in the Christian calendar is known as the Feast of Epiphany, a commemoration of the coming of the Magi to the stable in Bethlehem with their gifts of gold, frankincense and myrrh.

Shakespeare's title to his play, however, has nothing to do with its story and merely refers to when it was performed, probably 6 January 1602. It is likely that the alternative title, *What You Will*, also refers to the festive associations, a signal to the audience that the play is an entertainment for a special occasion.

Dramatic background

Shakespeare probably wrote *Twelfth Night* in 1601 – there are references in the play to events which had happened in or just before

that year. When Fabian says that Sir Andrew has 'sailed into the north of my lady's [Olivia's] opinion, where you will hang like an icicle on a Dutchman's beard' (III.2.24–6) he is referring to William Barent's voyage to the Arctic (1596–7); and the characterisation of Malvolio's smiling face by Maria, 'into more lines than is in the new map with the augmentation of the Indies' (III.2.76–7) is a reference to a map of the East Indies published in 1599–1600 noted for its many odd lines radiating out from the centre.

The plot of *Twelfth Night* comes from two probable sources: a short story called *The Historie of Apolonius and Silla* and the Italian play, *Gl'Ingannati* (The Deceived Ones), a comedy of mistaken identity with only incidental love interest. Whatever the source of the play, it is the conventions which defined Elizabethan **romantic comedy** that need to be borne in mind while studying *Twelfth Night*. A typical play might include the **stock characters** of:

- A cunning servant who motivates much of the action
- A pedant or hypocrite
- A pair of young lovers
- Twins

Confusions of identity were a common feature as was disguise, and transvestite disguise in particular. Because these elements were so common, Shakespeare's audience must have entered the theatre with their expectations clearly focused.

Malvolio and Puritanism

Twelfth Night was sometimes given the title *Malvolio* when it was subsequently performed in Shakespeare's day, such was the impression which this extraordinary character had on audiences. This impression, of course, is the result of the way Shakespeare has turned a character 'type' into a richly individualised portrait. Perhaps Malvolio is a caricature of the unpopular Sir William Knollys, Controller of Her Majesty's Household, in which case his treatment in the play would have special comic significance for the first Court audience; for the wider Elizabethan audience, it was the depiction of Malvolio as a Puritan that was relevant.

DID YOU KNOW?

The Puritans who disapproved of the theatre in general, were particularly scandalized by boys cross-dressing as women.

The Puritans were a religious group who had condemned theatres and other entertainments because they thought they had a corrupting influence. They thought plays contained too much sex and violence, and were unchristian and the cause of sin. They dressed plainly, disliked drinking and had a strict code of personal behaviour.

Many of the Puritans in Shakespeare's time were connected to the merchant classes and were considered to be self-serving hypocrites. Malvolio embodies all the attributes which the pleasure-seeking Elizabethan audience was predisposed to hate. There is no explicit sympathy for him in the play whatsoever. The joke against him is curtailed by Sir Toby out of self-interest, and Olivia's comment at the end that he has been 'notoriously abused' (IV.2.90) is a half-serious echo of Malvolio's own earlier, pretentious phrase. However, Malvolio's final threat of revenge reverberates beyond the immediate context of the play: the Puritans succeeded in closing down the theatres in 1642.

Think of some modern-day Malvolio who would like to impose their moral standards on everybody else.

Stage setting

Only a few simple stage properties were ever used in the Elizabethan theatre. The setting of each scene was created by a combination of words and music. When the sea captain tells Viola that 'This is Illyria, lady' (I.2.2) it would have been in front of an audience who were willing to let their imaginations be acted upon by language. The country of Illyria may have been an actual place (now a part of former Yugoslavia) but to the Elizabethan audience its name evoked an almost magical region, far away from the real world, where all the improbabilities of the story could be accepted.

EXAMINER'S SECRET

A distant setting is common to Elizabethan **romantic comedy.** Impress the examiner with references to other comedies that use a remote region for a setting.

The setting of *Twelfth Night* is relevant to its themes of love, disguise and deception. Two houses and formal gardens have to be imagined, within which the characters seem separated from one another by the preoccupations of their respective plots and the limitations of their own understanding. Beyond this the hostile, unfathomable sea roars, the sea which for Orsino is like the 'spirit of love' (I.1.9) and which has brought Viola and Sebastian to the shores of Illyria.

HOUSEHOLD OF ORSINO, DUKE OF ILLYRIA

Valentine
Curio
First officer
Second Officer

THE SHIPWRECKED

Viola and Sebastian

Captain and Antonio

HOUSEHOLD OF COUNTESS OLIVIA

Maria
Sir Toby Belch
Sir Andrew Aguecheek
Malvolio
Fabian
Feste

Viola : Shipwrecked on the coast of Illyria.
The Duke Orsino meets Viola who is now dressed as a man – Cesario. She falls in love with him.
Sebastian, Viola's brother is brought ashore on another part of the coast.

malvolio
Maria, Aguecheek and Sir Toby, plot to make a fool of malvolio.
Duke Orsino is in love with Olivia. However, Olivia falls in love with Cesario(viola).
All is revealed and Olivia marries Sebastian - The count marries viola.

TIMELINE

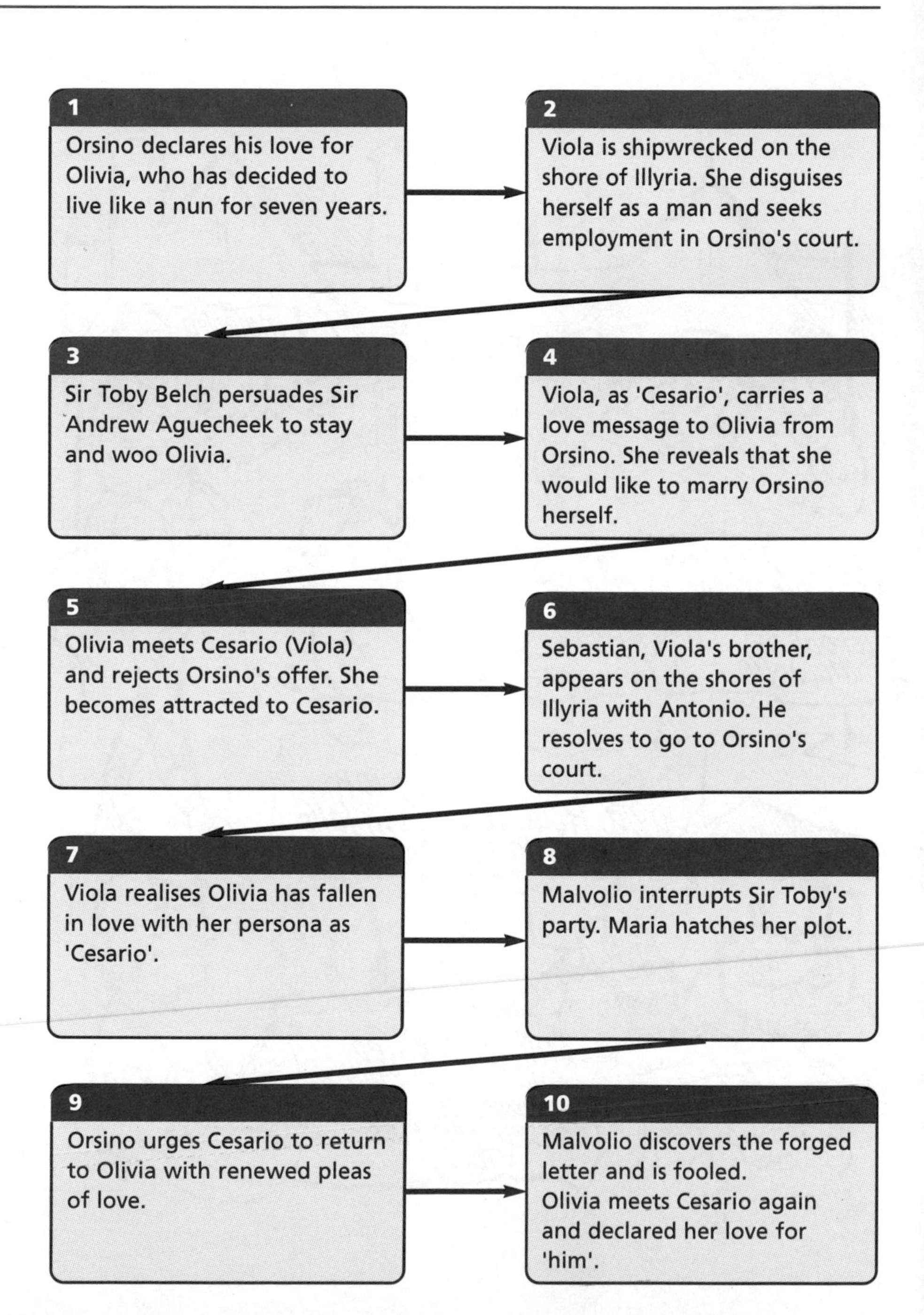
1
Orsino declares his love for Olivia, who has decided to live like a nun for seven years.
2
Viola is shipwrecked on the shore of Illyria. She disguises herself as a man and seeks employment in Orsino's court.
3
Sir Toby Belch persuades Sir Andrew Aguecheek to stay and woo Olivia.
4
Viola, as 'Cesario', carries a love message to Olivia from Orsino. She reveals that she would like to marry Orsino herself.
5
Olivia meets Cesario (Viola) and rejects Orsino's offer. She becomes attracted to Cesario.
6
Sebastian, Viola's brother, appears on the shores of Illyria with Antonio. He resolves to go to Orsino's court.
7
Viola realises Olivia has fallen in love with her persona as 'Cesario'.
8
Malvolio interrupts Sir Toby's party. Maria hatches her plot.
9
Orsino urges Cesario to return to Olivia with renewed pleas of love.
10
Malvolio discovers the forged letter and is fooled.
Olivia meets Cesario again and declared her love for 'him'.

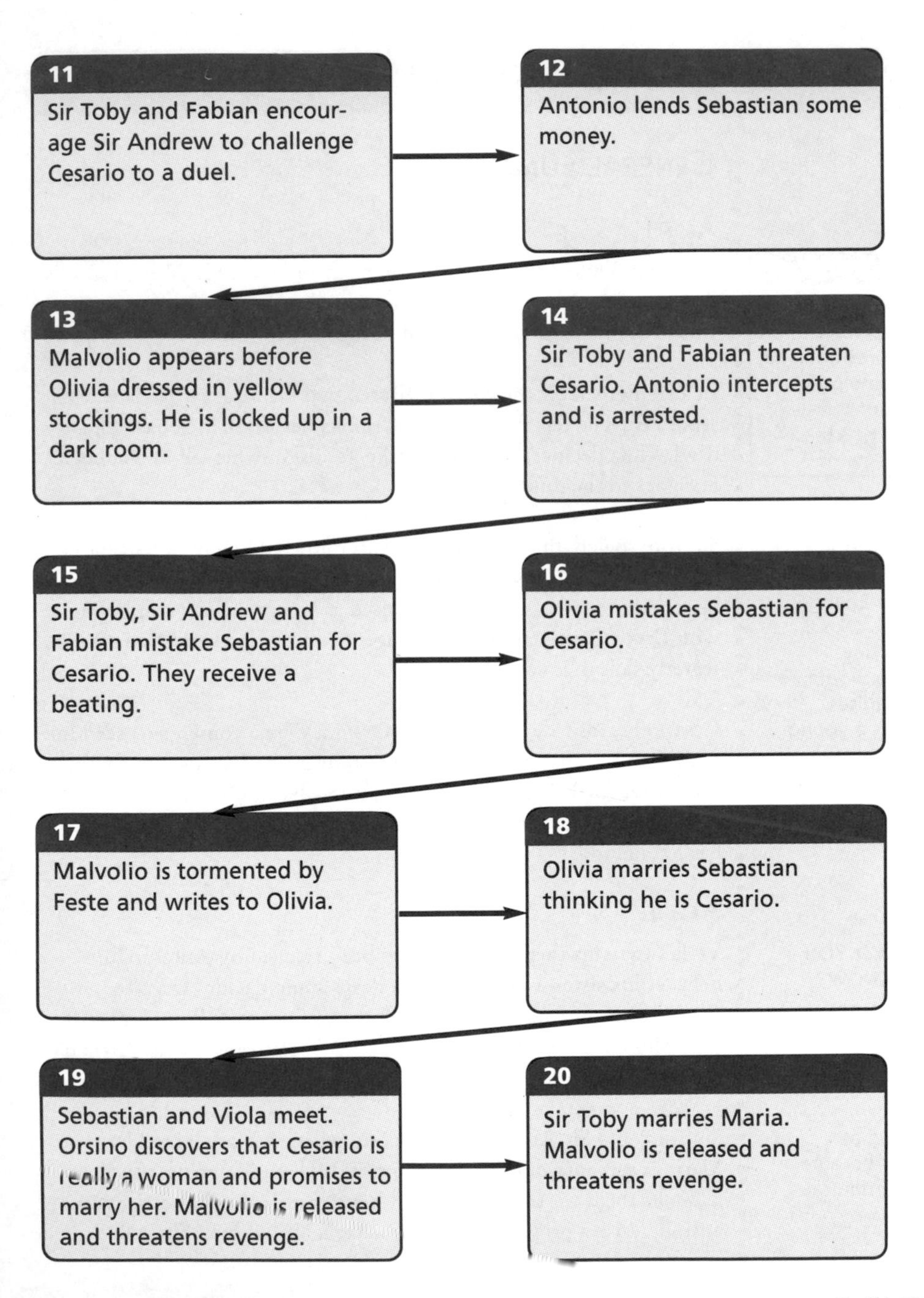
11
Sir Toby and Fabian encourage Sir Andrew to challenge Cesario to a duel.
12
Antonio lends Sebastian some money.
13
Malvolio appears before Olivia dressed in yellow stockings. He is locked up in a dark room.
14
Sir Toby and Fabian threaten Cesario. Antonio intercepts and is arrested.
15
Sir Toby, Sir Andrew and Fabian mistake Sebastian for Cesario. They receive a beating.
16
Olivia mistakes Sebastian for Cesario.
17
Malvolio is tormented by Feste and writes to Olivia.
18
Olivia marries Sebastian thinking he is Cesario.
19
Sebastian and Viola meet. Orsino discovers that Cesario is really a woman and promises to marry her. Malvolio is released and threatens revenge.
20
Sir Toby marries Maria. Malvolio is released and threatens revenge.

PART TWO

SUMMARIES

GENERAL SUMMARY

ACT I

In Illyria, Duke Orsino reflects on his love for Olivia. Valentine tells him that Olivia has vowed to mourn her brother's death for seven years. Orsino regards it as proof of her love for him!

CHECKPOINT 1

Viola and Sebastian are shipwrecked on the shores of Illyria. Find some other stories of the period which feature twins.

In a shipwreck off the coast of Illyria, two identical twins have been separated. The female twin, Viola, thinks her brother, Sebastian, is dead. Viola decides, for safety's sake, to disguise herself as a eunuch. She goes to the duke's court.

CHECK THE BOOK

Read the Epilogue to *As You Like It*, where a boy playing a woman who disguises herself as a young man reveals that he/she/he is really a woman.

Sir Toby Belch, the uncle of Olivia, is outraged by her decision to go into mourning. He wants his friend, Sir Andrew Aguecheek, to seek her hand in marriage. Viola (disguised as Cesario) finds employment with Duke Orsino as love-messenger between him and Olivia. Viola secretly falls in love with Orsino.

Cesario begins to woo Olivia for Orsino. Olivia consents to see him. Although she encourages Cesario to return, she forbids him to pursue the matter further. To make Cesario come back, Olivia sends Malvolio (her steward) after him with a ring which she pretends he has left behind.

ACT II

DID YOU KNOW?

The alehouse, where 'cakes and ale' (II.3.115) were served, became a centre for socialising as churches became more puritanical.

Viola's twin brother, Sebastian, has been rescued by Antonio but believes his sister is dead. He is in despair and decides to go to Orsino's court. Antonio, an old enemy of Orsino, follows him. After Malvolio has given the ring to 'Cesario', Viola realises that Olivia has fallen in love with 'him'.

Sir Toby and Sir Andrew are drinking when they are joined by Maria (a servant) and the clown, Feste. Malvolio interrupts them and tells them to stop the noise. Resentful of Malvolio's arrogant attitude, Maria proposes a plan to make a fool of him. She will

forge a love letter in Olivia's handwriting and leave it for Malvolio to find.

Meanwhile, Orsino finds he trusts and likes Cesario (Viola) greatly and tells the youth to convince Olivia of his love for her.

Malvolio imagines being married to his mistress. He finds Maria's forged letter and becomes convinced that Olivia loves him. In the letter he finds a love-poem and some instructions on how he should behave and dress.

ACT III

Olivia confesses to Cesario (Viola) that she has fallen in love with him but Cesario (Viola) rejects her.

Sir Andrew Aguecheek has spied Olivia and Cesario together and become jealous. He is persuaded to challenge Cesario to a duel.

On seeing the 'transformed' Malvolio, Olivia believes he has gone mad. He is locked up in a dark room.

Goaded and misled by Sir Toby and Fabian, Sir Andrew and Cesario (Viola) are brought together and forced to draw swords. Antonio enters. On seeing Cesario, he mistakenly believes it is Sebastian. He draws his sword and threatens to attack Sir Andrew and Sir Toby. Orsino's officers arrive and arrest him. Antonio addresses Cesario as 'Sebastian' and the disguised Viola begins to hope that her twin brother is alive.

ACT IV

Sebastian is mistaken for Cesario (Viola) and is attacked by Sir Andrew. Sebastian responds by beating the knight. Olivia appears and also assumes that Sebastian is Cesario and talks to him lovingly. She scolds her uncle for threatening to attack Sebastian. Olivia invites him in to her house and Sebastian follows her.

Malvolio has been imprisoned and Maria and Feste play a new trick on him. Feste dresses up as a priest, and torments him. Sir Toby

CHECK THE FILM

The film, *When Harry met Sally* (1989) is a modern romantic comedy which plays on the **genre's** tendency to prolong the making of the right match: the audience knows from the start that the couple will finally get together.

decides to bring the joke against Malvolio to an end and Feste agrees to help Malvolio explain to Olivia that he is not really mad.

Olivia summons a priest and marries Sebastian.

ACT V

EXAMINER'S SECRET
When writing about a specific scene or extract always make connections with the play as a whole – this at least shows you have read the complete work!

Orsino recognises Antonio who explains that he is not a pirate, and that he has rescued Sebastian, who (he believes) has disowned him just before he was arrested. He points accusingly at Cesario (Viola), thinking he is Sebastian.

Olivia appears and finally rejects Orsino, telling him that she has just married Cesario. Orsino threatens to kill Cesario, when Sir Andrew and Sir Toby appear claiming that Cesario (Viola) has assaulted them.

At last Sebastian enters and Viola (Cesario), recognising her lost brother, reveals her true identity. Olivia sends for Malvolio who learns the facts of his deception. He leaves, threatening revenge on all of them.

However, the play ends happily, for Sir Toby has married Maria, Olivia has married Sebastian, and the Duke Orsino promises to marry Viola.

Now take a break! 

CONTENTS

DETAILED SUMMARIES

SCENE 1 – Orsino in his palace

1. **Orsino talks about his love for Olivia.**
2. **Orsino is waiting for a reply to a message he has sent to Olivia.**
3. **Valentine tells him that she is in mourning for her dead brother.**

Orsino, Duke of Illyria, sits in his palace listening to music. He reflects on the many emotions that music inspires in people who are in love. The duke himself is in love with Olivia and his mood is sentimental and fanciful. He soon tires of the music and stops the musicians. He speaks of the 'spirit of love' (line 9), its excessive needs and fickleness. Notice the **simile** of the sea to describe the 'spirit of love' which is never satisfied. 'Receiveth as the sea, nought enters there, … / But falls into abatement and low price, / Even in a minute!' (lines 11–14). At the end of the play Orsino will quickly change his affections from Olivia to Viola (V.1.265–6). Orsino's page, Curio, tries to distract him and asks if he would like to go hunting.

The duke replies that he is already hunting the 'noblest' (line 18) prey – Olivia. He is waiting for a reply to a message he has sent to her. When Valentine, the messenger, enters he has some disappointing news. Olivia's brother has died and she has vowed to mourn his death for seven years, during which time no one will see her face. Orsino is not put off by this. On the contrary, he thinks that if Olivia 'hath a heart of that fine frame' (line 33) to mourn a brother, then she would be even more sensitive and loyal to him as a lover.

Two kinds of extreme emotion are presented in this opening scene: Orsino's passion for Olivia and Olivia's vow to mourn for seven years. This encourages the audience to wonder if these feelings will survive.

DID YOU KNOW?

The locations that appear at the head of scenes in modern editions of Shakespeare were added by editors in the eighteenth and nineteenth centuries, when stage traditions required realistic scenery on a 'picture-frame' stage.

CHECK THE FILM

The recent film by Trevor Nunn does not open with this scene. Think about the differences between drama on film and on stage.

GLOSSARY

abatement lowering

CHECKPOINT 2

How would you describe Orsino's character in this scene?

CHECK THE BOOK

John Dover Wilson has compiled an anthology of writings, *Life in Shakespeare's England* (Macmillan, 1913), from the Elizabethan era covering a wide range of relevant topics. This book is probably now only available in libraries.

The setting

The play is set in a remote distant place to intensify the romantic quality. Soft and sentimental music matches Orsino's musical language, so reflecting the theme of romance: 'If music be the food of love, play on, / Give me excess of it' (lines 1–2). We learn about Orsino's attitude to love in this scene: he is as much in love with Olivia as he is with the idea of love itself. This revelling in emotion makes him appear a rather passive lover.

SCENE 2 – Viola arrives at Illyria

1. **On the sea coast of Illyria, Viola, a sea captain and some sailors have recently survived a shipwreck.**
2. **The captain tells Viola that he saw her twin brother, Sebastian, being swept away by the waves.**
3. **The captain reveals that he was born and brought up nearby.**
4. **Viola decides to disguise herself as a man and go and serve the 'noble' Duke Orsino.**

On the sea coast of Illyria, Viola, a sea captain and some sailors have recently survived a shipwreck. The captain tells Viola that he saw her twin brother, Sebastian, tying himself to a mast just before the boat was split in two. The captain watched Sebastian being swept away by the waves and thinks that, although it is possible he survived, it is more likely that they are the only survivors.

Viola rewards the captain with gold because he has given her at least some hope. She asks him if he is familiar with the country they have landed in. He is, and says he was born and brought up 'Not three hours' travel from this very place' (line 23). Viola learns that Illyria is governed by the 'noble' (line 25) Duke Orsino whose name she remembers her late father mention. He was a bachelor in those days and according to the captain still is.

The captain has only just visited Illyria and heard that Orsino was seeking the love of the 'fair' (line 34) Olivia. Viola asks about Olivia and the captain tells her that she is a 'virtuous maid' (line 36) whose father died a year ago leaving her under the protection of a brother, who has also died recently. Since then she has turned her back on the world.

Viola wishes she could serve Olivia, perhaps because she herself is also brotherless. The captain tells her that would be impossible because Olivia will see no one.

There are similarities and differences between Viola and what we have learned about Olivia by this stage. They are both brotherless, both recently orphaned. Their names make an almost exact anagram. Yet Olivia can express her grief publicly and Viola cannot – she has to work out a way to survive.

CHECKPOINT 3

Apart from enabling Viola to protect herself in a strange land, what are the dramatic advantages of a disguised character? Why are there points of similarity between Olivia and Viola?

Viola devises a plan. She will serve the duke instead. She promises to pay the captain if he will help her disguise herself as a eunuch and then take her to Orsino. She can sing, and she plays many musical instruments; in this way she will make the duke employ her. The captain agrees to help her.

Viola's disguise begins a complicated series of concealments and confusions which continues throughout the play.

There is a reference to music in relation to the duke and Viola, perhaps suggesting that she and Orsino might eventually fall in love,

GLOSSARY

virtuous maid virgin

'for I can sing, / And speak to him in many sorts of music' (lines 57–8).

EXAMINER'S SECRET

Keep track of all the references to different sorts of disguise and concealment to be found in the play.

Appearance and reality

When Viola tells the captain that he has 'a mind that suits / With this thy fair and outward character' (lines 50–1) she is anticipating a major theme in the play. At different stages in the play few of the main characters are what they seem to be, including the morally good Viola.

SCENE 3 – Sir Andrew Aguecheek meets Maria

EXAMINER'S SECRET

Sir Toby's first line would be an excellent quote to use when trying to sum up his character and the things he stands for in the play.

1. **In Olivia's house, her uncle, Sir Toby Belch, is complaining about his niece's decision to retreat from the world.**
2. **Maria, Olivia's servant, complains of the 'foolish knight' (line 15) that Sir Toby has brought home to woo Olivia.**
3. **Sir Andrew appears and Sir Toby introduces the knight to Maria.**
4. **Sir Toby discovers that his friend is feeling very pessimistic about his chances with Olivia and is threatening to ride home the next day.**
5. **Sir Toby manages to persuade Aguecheek to stay for another month.**

The scene shifts to Olivia's house where her uncle, Sir Toby Belch, is complaining about the way his niece is mourning her brother's death.

He thinks she is over-reacting. Maria, Olivia's servant, tells him that Olivia disapproves of his late nights, his clothes and his drinking bouts. She has also complained of the 'foolish knight' that Sir Toby has brought home to woo her.

Sir Andrew Aguecheek is a stupid waster, says Maria, but Sir Toby will have none of it. Not only is Sir Andrew rich, he replies, but he can play the viola-di-gamba and speak three or four languages. Maria retorts that Sir Andrew is a fool, a quarreller, a coward and a drunkard. And just as Sir Toby is making the extravagant claim that all their drinking amounts to are a few toasts to Olivia, Sir Andrew appears.

Sir Toby introduces the knight to Maria, who proceeds to make him look every bit as stupid as she has claimed. She handles both Sir Toby and Sir Andrew with skill. She is clever at verbal sparring and her frank opinion of them suggests the influential role she will play in the comic **subplot** which is to follow.

After she has gone Sir Toby discovers that his friend is feeling very pessimistic about his chances with Olivia and is threatening to ride home the next day. She will see no one, he says, and even if she did, she certainly would not want to have anything to do with him. Besides, adds Sir Andrew, the Count Orsino is wooing her.

Sir Toby manages to persuade Aguecheek to stay for another month by telling him that he has heard Olivia say she would never marry an older, more intelligent and more important person than herself.

Sir Toby prompts Sir Andrew to admit that he is a good dancer. They will have a lot of fun if he stays and shows off his steps. The two knights agree to continue their 'revels' (line 134).

It's obvious that Sir Andrew is Sir Toby's dupe. The 'three thousand ducats a year' (line 22) is a significant factor in their relationship because Sir Andrew finances Sir Toby's pleasures and must be kept happy.

CHECKPOINT 4

Think about Sir Toby's relationship to Olivia, Maria and Sir Andrew from what is given in this scene.

New characters

A new set of characters is introduced and the play moves from a romantic world down to a more earthy, fun-loving one of 'downstairs' characters.

Sir Toby's explosive first line, 'What a plague means my niece to take the death of her brother thus? I am sure care's an enemy to life' (lines 1–3) reveals his relationship to Olivia and the kind of character he is – a man devoted to pleasure.

GLOSSARY

ducat gold coin

Olivia now has two suitors: Duke Orsino and the ridiculous Sir Andrew Aguecheek, and Malvolio will later make a third. The comic subplot reflects the main plot.

SCENE 4 – Viola at the court of Duke Orsino

1. **Valentine tells 'Cesario' (Viola) that he is Orsino's favourite already.**
2. **Orsino instructs 'Cesario' to take a message to Olivia.**
3. **Viola admits she has feelings for Orsino.**

EXAMINER'S SECRET

Don't write all you know about a subject, whatever the question. Focus on three or four topics in order of importance and relevance to the question.

This is the first time we see Viola as 'Cesario'. Disguised as the eunuch, she has become a great favourite with the Duke Orsino, even though he has known Cesario for only three days.

There is a sharp contrast between Orsino as a suitor for Olivia and Sir Andrew in the previous scene. The duke can't help but look good against the absurd knight.

Taking Cesario aside, Orsino commands him to carry love messages to Olivia. He urges the youth to be persistent, even to the point of discourtesy, until Olivia agrees to receive him. Cesario must describe to Olivia, Orsino's passion and his sorrow. The extent of Orsino's confidence in Cesario is clear from the way he dismisses the other courtiers so that they can be alone together. Orsino regards Cesario more as an intimate friend than a mere servant. This anticipates and makes possible their later relationship.

The duke believes that because Cesario is so young and handsome – looking and sounding almost like a young girl himself – Olivia is more likely to respond favourably, 'It shall become thee well to act my woes: / She will attend it better in thy youth' (lines 26–7). Cesario will be rewarded well if he is successful.

You need to be aware of the idea of **dramatic irony** in this scene: when the duke speaks admiringly of Cesario's feminine appearance and promises that he shall 'live as freely as thy lord' (line 39) he speaks more than he knows.

In a revealing aside, Cesario (Viola) bemoans a situation in which she will be wooing for a man whom she herself would like to marry '... yet, a barful strife! / Whoe'er I woo, myself would be his wife' (lines 41–2). Viola's declaration that she herself loves the duke also prepares the audience for the ending. Yet one word, 'barful' (line 41), indicates her awareness of the problems which this love has yet to encounter before its fulfilment.

DID YOU KNOW?

The first recorded reference to the play *Twelfth Night* was in a letter written in 1601 by an Italian Duke (Orsino!) who saw Shakespeare's company perform it at court.

SCENE 5 – Olivia meets Cesario

1. **Feste is told off by Maria for disappearing.**
2. **Feste tries to amuse Olivia and succeeds.**
3. **Malvolio insults Feste.**
4. **Cesario comes with his message for Olivia.**
5. **Olivia falls for Cesario.**

In Olivia's house Maria is telling Feste, the clown, that Olivia is annoyed by his absence. She wants to know where he has been and jokes that Olivia will hang him for playing truant. Feste does not care. 'Many a good hanging prevents a bad marriage' (line 19), he says.

Maria advises him to have a good excuse prepared because Olivia is about to appear.

Olivia enters, accompanied by her steward, Malvolio. She is very solemn and in no mood to listen to the prattling clown. She orders him away, but Feste embarks on some joking that eventually amuses her. His attempt to prove Olivia is a fool (lines 55–70) by mocking her state of mourning anticipates her behaviour later in the scene.

Malvolio, however, finds the clown's joking impertinent and humourless. He wonders why Olivia finds such pleasure in someone so feeble in mind and body. Olivia responds by reproving Malvolio for his pride and intolerance. There is no offence in Feste's joking, she says, because he is an 'allowed fool' (line 93), permitted to make

GLOSSARY

barful full of hindrances

CHECK THE BOOK

Compare other 'clowns' in Shakespeare's plays, such as *King Lear, The Winter's Tale* and *As You Like It*.

harmless jests. Her description of Malvolio's character 'O, you are sick of self-love, Malvolio, and taste with a distempered appetite' (lines 89–90) is meant to stick in our minds. He is depicted as an enemy of pleasure and wit who takes himself and everybody else too seriously. This prepares the audience for the trick that will be played on him later.

Olivia is clearly intelligent – she appreciates the punning wit of the clown and her characterisation of Malvolio is very accurate.

Maria announces that a handsome young gentleman has arrived who wishes to speak with Olivia, but he is being delayed at the gate by Sir Toby Belch. Olivia instructs Maria to fetch her uncle away, since he will be talking nothing but rubbish.

CHECKPOINT 5

How does Shakespeare build up a picture of Olivia's character and situation in this scene?

While Maria and Malvolio are off-stage Sir Toby enters, drunk, and his niece tries to find out who the 'gentleman' is. But her uncle is too drunk to make sense; when he has stumbled off Olivia sends Feste to look after him.

Malvolio returns and informs Olivia that the young man insists on speaking to her. He will accept no excuses. Olivia asks what sort of man he is and is told that he is young and handsome, with a sharp voice. Olivia relents. She will see him but only in the presence of Maria, who is instructed to veil Olivia's face.

CHECKPOINT 6

Which details prepare the audience for what is to come?

When Cesario (Viola) enters he embarks on his mission with a series of compliments, while cleverly avoiding Olivia's questions about himself. It is clear that Olivia is very interested in this handsome youth, but he will not tell her his message while other people are present.

Olivia dismisses Maria and the attendants.

The conversation between Olivia and Cesario starts off in **prose** and moves to the **poetic** form of **blank verse** to emphasise the dialogue's focus on the subject of love. Cesario tells Olivia that his message comes from Orsino's heart and he asks to see her face. When she unveils herself Cesario is full of admiration, regretting that the owner of such beauty should be so cruel as to never have children and thus 'leave the world no copy' (line 246). Don't worry, replies Olivia, I will leave an account of my beauty in writing when I die; every aspect of it will be written down.

EXAMINER'S SECRET

When writing about this scene, you will impress the marker if you refer to similar attitudes to love, beauty and mortality found in Shakespeare's sonnets.

When Cesario tells Olivia that Orsino loves her 'With adoration, fertile tears, / With groans that thunder love, with sighs of fire' (lines 259–60) he is using an exaggerated form of language known as **hyperbole** which is common to love poetry. Perhaps there is an element of Viola's own feelings for Orsino here, and in the 'willow cabin' speech (lines 272–80).

In spite of Cesario's affirmation that Orsino truly loves her, Olivia says she cannot love him in return, despite all his virtues. (The irrational nature of love is a major theme of the play.) He must not continue his suit. Yet if Cesario would like to return, Olivia will be happy to see him. The audience becomes aware of Olivia's love for Cesario in this part of the scene. She tries to pay him, but Cesario proudly declines to accept the gold he is offered and leaves.

Olivia cannot love Orsino (lines 261–6), yet she is amazed at how quickly she has fallen for Cesario (line 299). By now infatuated with someone she believes is a handsome young man, Olivia recalls Malvolio and tells him to follow the messenger with a ring which she

Scene 5 continued

claims he has left behind. She asks Malvolio to tell Cesario that if he returns tomorrow she will provide more reasons for her refusal of the duke.

At the close of the scene Olivia has fallen in love with Cesario, the duke's go-between. The ring is a ruse to make him return.

DID YOU KNOW?

People in Elizabethan and Jacobean times did not speak like the characters in Shakespeare's plays. He wrote the way he did for poetic and dramatic reasons.

The problems begin

At the end of Act I Orsino loves Olivia who loves Cesario (Viola) who secretly loves Orsino. We find out about Olivia's capacity for self-deception in the rapid way she forgets her vows and allows herself to become so attracted to Cesario. This problem provides the impetus for the rest of the plot and its resolution. It creates a basic dramatic irony in which the audience knows more than the characters.

Now take a break!

WHO SAYS ...?

1 'O spirit of love, how quick and fresh art thou'

....

2 'like a cloistress she will veiled walk'

....

3 'A virtuous maid, the daughter of a count / That died some twelvemonth since; then leaving her / In the protection of his son, her brother, / Who shortly also died'

....

4 'I'll serve this duke; / Thou shalt present me as an eunuch to him'

....

5 'What a plague means my niece to take the death of her brother thus? I am sure care's an enemy to life.'

....

ABOUT WHOM?

6 'He's a very fool and a prodigal.'

....

7 'O, you are sick of self-love'

....

8 'Yet I suppose him virtuous, know him noble'

....

Check your answers on p. 97.

SCENE 1 – Enter Sebastian

1. **Sebastian and the sea captain, Antonio, are washed ashore.**
2. **Sebastian tells Antonio about his twin sister, Viola.**
3. **Sebastian makes off for Orsino's court, followed by Antonio.**

On the sea coast of Illyria we discover that Viola's twin brother, Sebastian, has not drowned after all. He was rescued from the sea by Antonio, another sea captain, who has been looking after him.

Sebastian is very unhappy; he is convinced Viola has drowned in the shipwreck. Antonio is keen to help him but Sebastian wants to be alone with his grief. He feels his misfortune is the result of an unlucky star and if Antonio joins forces with him, then Antonio himself might also be afflicted – 'the malignancy of my fate might perhaps distemper yours' (lines 4–5).

Yet Sebastian trusts Antonio and tells him something about himself and his background, in particular his beautiful twin sister who resembled him so much. Antonio is moved to pity by this and regrets that he may not have entertained Sebastian well enough. He asks if he could be his servant. Sebastian declines with elaborate courtesy; he cannot stand being a burden to Antonio any longer. He tells him he is going to Orsino's court and says goodbye.

CHECKPOINT 7

Compare this scene to Act I Scene 2. How does Sebastian differ from Viola in the same situation?

Although Antonio has many dangerous enemies in Orsino's court, his affection and concern for Sebastian are so great that, after he has gone, he decides to follow him there.

The role of Sebastian

The appearance of Sebastian, whom the now disguised Viola believes drowned, anticipates the comic complications of mistaken identity in Act V; he will be mistaken for Cesario (Viola), and Viola (as Cesario) will be mistaken for Sebastian. Sebastian is an attractive figure who commands respect and love, which is reflected in Antonio's decision to follow him.

SCENE 2 – Viola's problem

1 Malvolio tries to return Cesario's ring, telling him that Olivia is not interested in Orsino.

2 Viola reflects on the problem that has arisen.

This scene continues the action which started at the end of Act I.

Cesario (Viola) is followed by Malvolio who asks him if he is the same person who was recently with the Countess Olivia. Cesario replies that he is.

Malvolio proffers the ring which he has been told to return to the youth. Malvolio tells him sarcastically that he would have been spared the trouble of returning it to Cesario if Cesario had not been so forgetful.

With great contempt Malvolio relates what Olivia wishes Cesario to tell Orsino. He is to make it clear that she will have nothing to do with the duke. Cesario must never return with any more of Orsino's messages, except if it be to report to Olivia how Orsino took this rejection.

Malvolio's character is even more explicitly arrogant and scornful here. Part of the purpose is to bring this out so that the audience will be pleased when the trick is played on him. He despises anyone who is not above him socially.

Cesario is put off by Malvolio's manner and refuses the ring: 'I'll none of it' (line 11). The outraged Malvolio flings the ring to the ground and departs.

Viola reflects on what has happened. Since she certainly left no ring with Olivia, she fears that her appearance has taken in the countess: 'Fortune forbid my outside have not charm'd her!' (line 17). She is appalled to remember the details of her interview with Olivia, how she spoke in fits and starts, her vague distracted manner. All the evidence points her to the conclusion that Olivia has fallen in love with 'Cesario'. Obviously sending the 'churlish' (line 22) Malvolio

DID YOU KNOW?

Several of Shakespeare's plays, particularly the comedies, capitalize on the effect of boys acting as women who then take on disguise as boys. Boy actors could be apprenticed to a mature actor, who would teach them the art of performance.

GLOSSARY

distemper infect
outside appearance

with the ring was a trick to lure the messenger back.

Viola feels pity for Olivia. The lady might just as well 'love a dream' (line 25) as a woman disguised as a man. She declares that her disguise is 'a wickedness' (line 26), the work of the devil. Viola laments how easy it is for attractive but dishonest suitors to impress women's 'waxen hearts' (line 29). Viola is a woman, like Olivia, and women are shown as frail and impressionable.

CHECKPOINT 8

How does the fact that we have just met Sebastian makes us confident that 'time' will indeed provide a solution.

Finally, she expresses the terribly complex situation which has arisen: Viola loves Orsino, her master, as much as he loves Olivia; Olivia mistakenly dotes on Cesario, who is really a woman, Viola. She cannot think of a solution. She calls on time to unravel this 'hard … knot' (line 40) and the scene ends. This soliloquy is important. It allows her to express her feelings directly to the audience and to sum up the basic problem which the rest of the play has to resolve.

SCENE 3 – The party

1. **Sir Toby and Sir Andrew have a late-night drinking session.**
2. **Feste arrives and sings a song.**
3. **Sir Toby, Sir Andrew and Feste sing together very loudly.**
4. **Malvolio interrupts them and tells them off for making so much noise, threatening to report Maria to Olivia.**
5. **Maria devises her plan to make a fool of Malvolio.**

Late at night in Olivia's house Sir Toby Belch and Sir Andrew Aguecheek are having a drinking session. We learn that Sir Toby is not just an ordinary wisecracking drunkard: he is a man of some wit and learning, which comes through even though he is drunk. His characteristic form of wit is the quibble – playing on words which are ambiguous.

Their drunken conversation consists at first of a wildly absurd piece of reasoning prompted by Sir Toby, in which he tries to justify their late hours. To be up after midnight, he says, is to be up early 'and *diluculo surgere*, thou know'st' (lines 2–3) – (to rise early is very healthy). Sir Toby pursues the argument until the 'scholar' Sir Andrew concludes that life 'consists of eating and drinking' (lines 11–12). So let us eat and drink, agrees Sir Toby, calling Maria for some more wine.

Feste, the clown, is also up late and he enters, adding to the scene of broad comedy his own brand of word-play and nonsense. Sir Andrew is delighted with the clown's fooling, and knowing he has a sweet voice asks him to sing. Sir Toby requests a love song.

Feste's song

The clown's song is a point of seriousness in the scene. It announces the play's main theme of love and contrasts with the raucous part-songs which, in turn, are contrasted by the music of the following scene featuring the Duke Orsino and Viola.

Feste sings a song, 'O Mistress Mine', that urges young lovers to live for the moment and not delay their lovemaking; the future is always uncertain and youth does not last.

These sentiments and Feste's beautiful voice please Sir Toby and Sir Andrew greatly. After some more verbal knockabout, the three decide to sing together a catch, a piece of music where one part follows another. 'I am dog at a catch' (lines 62–3), cries Sir Andrew happily.

DID YOU KNOW?

When writing about this important scene, make sure you cover all the different elements which contribute to the comedy as a piece of physical theatre.

GLOSSARY

waxen receptoive

They make a terrible sound and Maria rushes in to complain at their 'caterwauling' (line 73). If Olivia is woken up by the noise she will have Malvolio throw them out of the house.

Maria's entreaties are ignored by the revellers who are too drunk to take anything or anybody seriously. Sir Toby dubs Malvolio a 'Peg-a-Ramsey' (line 77), that is, a spoil-sport, and just as he begins a new song, 'On the Twelfth Day of December', an indignant Malvolio appears.

Olivia's steward scolds them for their lack of manners and respect for others, and for making a vulgar ale-house out of his mistress's home.

Malvolio accuses Sir Toby Belch and his gang of keeping his mistress awake: 'Do ye make an ale-house of my lady's house, that ye squeak out your coziers' catches without any mitigation or remorse of voice?' (lines 89–92). Shakespeare captures the typical speech of a Puritan in this pedantic speech, modelled on the rhythms of the Bible.

CHECKPOINT 9

Does Malvolio's speech reflect his character? How?

Malvolio has been instructed by Olivia to tell Sir Toby that although he is her relative, she cannot tolerate his disorderly ways. If he will not stop this rowdiness he must leave at once. Malvolio is roundly mocked for this by Sir Toby and Feste, who relentlessly continue their singing. They think that Malvolio's high-handed sanctimonious manner is intolerable.

We are given a statement of the basic conflict between Sir Toby's values and those of Malvolio: 'Dost thou think, because thou art virtuous, there shall be no more cake and ale?' (lines 114–15). Sir Toby and his friends stand for a tolerant pleasure-loving view of life, and Malvolio stands for the puritanical denial of pleasure.

DID YOU KNOW?

Puritans hated all kinds of unrestrained entertainments. They dressed in simple black garments. Look up some pictures of typical Puritans.

Before he goes off, the scandalised steward assures Maria that he will be reporting her part in the unruliness to her mistress. Maria responds to his parting shot with scorn – 'Go shake your ears' (line 124) – and proposes a plan to make the pompous Malvolio look a fool.

She reveals that she will forge a love letter in Olivia's handwriting, which is often mistaken for hers, and this letter will contain an admiring description of Malvolio, 'the colour of his beard, the shape of his leg, the manner of his gait, the expressure of his eye, forehead, and complexion' (lines 156–8). Malvolio will find it and foolishly believe that Olivia is in love with him. Maria knows she can accomplish the trick and she suggests that the two knights spy on Malvolio 'where he shall find the letter' (lines 174–5) to watch how he interprets it.

Maria reveals her reasons to get even with Malvolio quite explicitly (line 146 onwards). Her analysis of Malvolio's psychology is penetrating. Shakespeare is presenting a viewpoint which he wants the audience to share while at the same time demonstrating Maria's sharpness of mind.

Sir Toby and Sir Andrew are delighted at the prospect of this opportunity to bring down Malvolio. They think Maria is an excellent woman and she certainly 'adores' (line 179) Sir Toby, who once more encourages Sir Andrew to believe he will have Olivia. Deciding it is too late to go to bed, Sir Toby leads Sir Andrew off in search of more wine.

CHECKPOINT 10

The **subplot** now develops and Malvolio is built up further as a thoroughly unsympathetic character. Summarise the revellers' objections to Malvolio.

SCENE 4 – Orsino and Cesario talk about love

1. **Orsino sends for Feste to sing a song.**
2. **Orsino gives some advice to Cesario on the subject of love.**
3. **Feste sings his song.**
4. **Orsino instructs Cesario to return to Olivia. He delivers his opinion on the worth of a woman's love.**
5. **Cesario (Viola) tells Orsino that women can love as well as men.**

This scene provides a strong contrast to the previous one and the change of mood is established as much by music – the 'caterwauling' (II.3.73) in Olivia's house and the 'old and antic' (line 3) song in Orsino's – as by the seriousness of the conversation between Orsino and Cesario. This is the first time we see Viola and Orsino together

GLOSSARY

coziers' catches cobblers' or tinkers' rounds

after her confession that she loves him (Act I Scene 4).

Duke Orsino is with his courtiers in his palace. He calls for music to be played. He tells Cesario that he would particularly like to hear a song that was performed during the previous evening. 'That old and antic song' (line 3) seemed to soothe his emotions far more than any of the superficial songs of the present time. Curio is sent to bring Feste, the clown, to sing and while they are waiting the duke talks to Cesario against a background of the old tune played by the musicians.

The duke tells Cesario to remember him if he should ever fall in love. For he, Orsino, is the typical true lover, lively and playful in all emotions except when he has in mind the 'constant image' (line 19) of his beloved. Cesario hints that he himself already knows something about what it means to love. The duke becomes curious about the woman who has attracted him. He questions the youth about what she is like, her appearance and age.

CHECKPOINT 11

Viola's disguise has created a strong **dramatic irony**: read the scene from Orsino's point of view and then from the audience's. What might an audience anticipate?

Cesario says that the woman is very like Orsino, both in temperament and age. Orsino is scornful: this woman is certainly too old. A woman should take an older man, he advises, because women by their nature become emotionally mature earlier than men. An older man is more likely to satisfy their needs. We young men may think highly of ourselves in love, he says, but our emotions are unstable, 'more giddy and unfirm' (line 33), more easily worn out than those of women.

Orsino recommends Cesario find himself a virgin in the first bloom of youthful beauty. She will keep his love alive for longer. Cesario agrees.

Curio returns with Feste and Orsino instructs the clown to sing the song. He tells Cesario to note that the song is 'old and plain' (line 43) and used to be sung by both old women and carefree young maids. The simple truth of its theme is the innocence of love.

The fact that Feste sings a song in both locations provides continuity and also points to Feste's independence, the 'allowed fool' (I.5.93) who is free to move and speak where he will.

The lover in this melancholy song is a young man whose heart has been broken by a *'fair cruel maid'* (line 54). He wishes to die and be buried without friends or other mourners so that no one will know where his bones are laid, *'O where / Sad true lover never find my grave, / To weep there'* (lines 64–6). Clearly the deep sadness of the song reflects the duke's mood; he is pleased with Feste's performance and pays him for it. Feste draws attention to Orsino's 'changeable' nature (lines 73–4) and this quality influences the duke's subsequent reflections on love.

Everybody except the duke and Cesario leave and Orsino tells him that he must return to Olivia and convince her that his love for her is truly noble. He is not impressed by Olivia's wealth and possessions – his soul loves her for what nature has made her, 'that miracle and queen of gems' (line 86), her beauty. And what, asks Cesario, if she cannot love you? Orsino replies that he will not be refused.

Cesario tells Orsino that he must accept her refusal. After all, if the duke were the object of some lady's passion, and he did not love her in return, he would be forced to tell her and expect her to accept it.

Orsino does not believe that women can love as passionately as men. He thinks women simply do not have the physical capacity to retain deep feeling; they quickly become sick of love by being too greedy for it in the first place.

Orsino's love, by comparison, is 'as hungry as the sea' (line 101) and like the deep ocean can absorb far more. He insists that there is no comparison between the love any woman could feel for him and the feelings he has for Olivia.

Cesario replies that he knows only too well how much women are able to love men. Women, he says, are 'as true of heart as we' (line 107). He knows this because his father had a daughter who loved a man quite as much as he might love Orsino if he, Cesario, were a woman.

Orsino asks what happened to the girl. She 'never told her love' (line 111), says Cesario, but pined away concealing her feelings from

CHECK THE BOOK

Look at Shakespeare's narrative poems, 'Venus and Adonis' and 'The Rape of Lucrece' to find out more about his deep interest in the themes of love and sexual desire.

CHECKPOINT 12

How does Shakespeare communicate the depth of Viola's love for Orsino?

GLOSSARY

antic old

CHECKPOINT 13

Look at the way the scene is constructed.

her beloved, so intensely that her concealed love consumed all her youth. He tells Orsino that 'we' men may talk a lot about our feelings, but we profess more than we actually feel. And, Orsino asks, did your sister die of her love? Cesario answers with a riddle: 'I am all the daughters of my father's house, / And all the brothers too' (lines 121–2). On this mysterious note the scene ends. Orsino dispatches Cesario to Olivia. He is to tell her that the duke's love cannot be denied.

The ending of the scene moves the plot on further, anticipating another meeting between Olivia and Cesario (Viola).

Viola tries to convey her true feelings

We are more interested in Viola's emotions here than in Orsino's. A tension is created between her 'fictional' role as the man, Cesario, and the real feelings she tries to express indirectly as a woman who is secretly in love with Orsino. The true pathos of Viola's situation is given, yet this is qualified by the irony created by Orsino's ignorance of 'Cesario's' true identity and the way Shakespeare is developing an increasingly intimate relationship between them.

SCENE 5 – THE GULLING OF MALVOLIO

1. **Sir Toby, Sir Andrew and Fabian hide in the garden to watch Malvolio find the forged letter.**
2. **Malvolio enters, deeply engrossed in fantasies about Olivia.**
3. **He finds the letter and is thrilled to believe that Olivia loves him.**
4. **After Malvolio has gone, the onlookers emerge, delighted with the success of their trick.**

DID YOU KNOW?

Bear baiting was a popular sport of the Elizabethans, and especially the kind of people who attended the theatre.

This scene provides another strong contrast and takes us back again into the comic subplot, the gulling of Malvolio. We meet a new character, Fabian, who offers a further reason for the attack on Malvolio's vanity and sanctimoniousness: the steward has reported him for bear baiting, a sport much disapproved of by Puritans.

In Olivia's garden Sir Toby, Sir Andrew and Fabian, meet together in anticipation of the trick they are playing on Malvolio.

Maria arrives with the 'bait', the forged letter, and she tells them to hide themselves in the 'box-tree' (line 15).

Malvolio enters and he is a character who is ripe for mockery. His conceit makes him an easy target for the tricksters. And it is this conceit, combined with his egotistical pretensions, which makes the trick possible. He is engrossed in thoughts of Olivia and the possibility that she might love him. 'Maria once told me she did affect me, and I have heard herself come thus near, that should she fancy, it should be one of my complexion' (lines 23–6).

To the indignation of the eavesdroppers, Malvolio proceeds to fantasise about being married to Olivia, being 'Count Malvolio' (line 35). After all, there has been an instance when a noble lady married one of her servants. The dramatic convention of **soliloquy**, where a character speaks his/her thoughts alone, is exploited to full comic effect here.

Malvolio has no difficulty picturing himself as a loving husband, dressed in velvet, surrounded by servants who would defer to his authoritative manner. And it would be a special pleasure to be able to summon Sir Toby Belch and remind him that he now has the right to give him orders. He would instruct Olivia's uncle to give up his drunkenness and tell him that he is wasting too much time with a foolish knight, 'One Sir Andrew' (line 80).

Then Malvolio catches sight of the letter. He picks it up and begins to read it out loud, utterly convinced it is in Olivia's handwriting. The phrases used in the letter are typical of Olivia and the note has her stamp, so it must be from her.

There is a love poem inside and the first verse says that only God knows the man whom the writer loves and she must tell no one who it is. If only this person were Malvolio! The second verse prompts him to believe it is him because Olivia writes '*I may command where I adore*' (line 106). He, after all, is her steward and she may command

CHECKPOINT 14

What is Malvolio feeling when he finds the letter?

EXAMINER'S SECRET

Don't just 'tell the story' of this scene – imagine the gestures and expressions of the actors as Malvolio reads the letter. Try to convey the sense of comedy experienced by a real audience.

GLOSSARY

affect: fancy

him: 'I serve her, she is my lady' (line 117). The first part is all quite logical, but what of the letters M.O.A.I. which end the poem? Malvolio soon takes them to signify him, since all the letters are in his name.

Malvolio then finds a prose letter enclosed with the poem. It is this letter that finally convinces him that Olivia loves him.

The letter says that if it should by chance fall into her beloved's hands, then he should consider the fact that the woman who loves him is, through fate, socially his superior. He should not be afraid of this 'greatness' – '*Some are born great, some achieve greatness, and some have greatness thrust upon 'em*' (lines 145–6).

DID YOU KNOW?

Yellow stockings and cross garters would have been considered laughably unfashionable by the Elizabethan audience.

The author of the letter writes that Fate calls on him to take the initiative for he is being made a very generous offer. He should be bold, cast off his usual clothes and start wearing yellow stockings and cross garters. He should be rude to servants and go about talking of important, high-flown subjects. Unless he does all these things he will still be thought of as a mere steward, a servant who is '*not worthy to touch Fortune's fingers*' (lines 156–7). The letter is signed '*The Fortunate Unhappy*' (line 159), a typical Elizabethan **oxymoron** – a paradox that combines one idea with its opposite.

Malvolio is overjoyed after reading this letter. He tells himself he will do all that has been 'commended' (line 166). He will be 'proud' (line 161), he will treat Sir Toby with contempt. He will have nothing to do with common people. He will be exactly the man described in the letter. For it is as clear as daylight that Olivia wrote it. Nothing makes this plainer than the reference to yellow stockings and cross garters, for Olivia has recently admired his stockings and obviously wants him to continue the habit.

A postscript to the letter which Malvolio reads out contains more encouragement. It says that by now he must surely realise who the writer is. If he is prepared to love her, he should show this by smiling in her presence, smiling all the time.

You will find on-line versions of Shakespeare's plays at **http://www.bartleby.com**

Malvolio is thoroughly fooled

Maria has obviously conceived the letter knowing very well what her mistress dislikes, and she clearly understands Malvolio's character as well in the way the letter plays upon his weaknesses.

The audience is made to anticipate future events in this scene, in particular through the expectation of an hilarious encounter between Malvolio and Olivia (Act III Scene 4).

Malvolio exits. Sir Toby, Sir Andrew and Fabian emerge from their hiding place. Soon Maria returns to join them.

They are all very pleased with the trick which she has played on Malvolio. Sir Toby is full of admiration and claims he would marry her and 'ask no other dowry … but such another jest' (lines 184–5). He tells Maria that with this demonstration of her cleverness she has completely conquered him.

Maria tells them that if they want to see the 'fruits of the sport' (line 197) they must watch for Malvolio's next encounter with Olivia. He is sure to appear in yellow stockings (a colour she hates) and cross garters ('a fashion she detests' – line 200). Malvolio's endless smiling is bound to make the melancholic Olivia extremely annoyed.

The hoaxers all go off looking forward to Malvolio's humiliation.

GLOSSARY

dowry: a gift given for a wife at marriage

Test yourself (Act II)

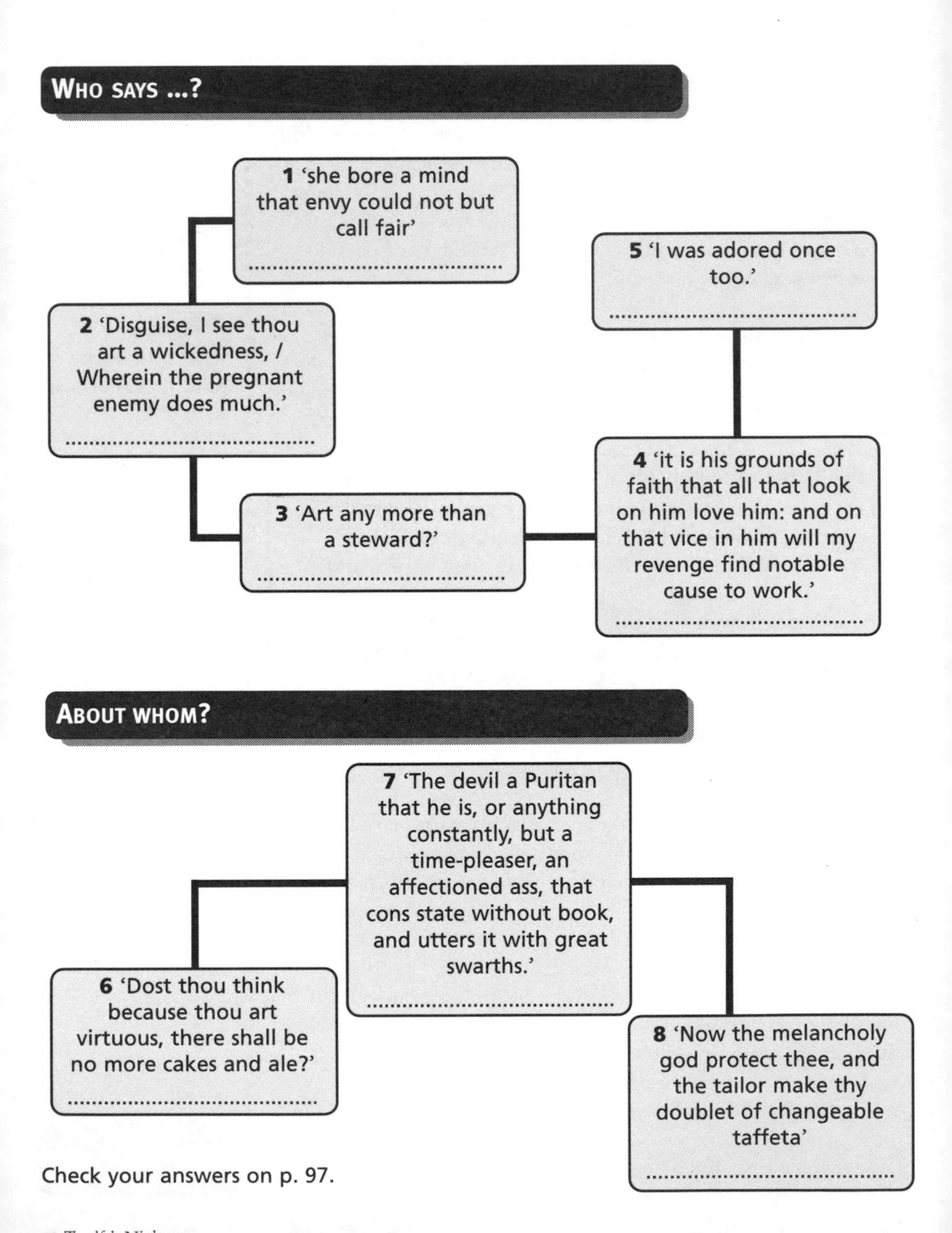

Who says ...?

1 'she bore a mind that envy could not but call fair'

....

2 'Disguise, I see thou art a wickedness, / Wherein the pregnant enemy does much.'

....

3 'Art any more than a steward?'

....

4 'it is his grounds of faith that all that look on him love him: and on that vice in him will my revenge find notable cause to work.'

....

5 'I was adored once too.'

....

About whom?

6 'Dost thou think because thou art virtuous, there shall be no more cakes and ale?'

....

7 'The devil a Puritan that he is, or anything constantly, but a time-pleaser, an affectioned ass, that cons state without book, and utters it with great swarths.'

....

8 'Now the melancholy god protect thee, and the tailor make thy doublet of changeable taffeta'

....

Check your answers on p. 97.

SCENE 1 – Olivia meets Cesario again

1. **Cesario (Viola) returns to Olivia's house and talks to Feste.**
2. **Sir Toby and Sir Andrew meet Cesario.**
3. **Olivia tells Cesario that she loves him.**

In the garden Cesario meets Feste, the clown, who is playing on the pipe and drum. They indulge in some light-hearted witty conversation and Feste's wit provides a lively start to the Act.

Cesario points out that people who play so cleverly with words, as Feste does, may soon give them lewd double meanings. He asks Feste if he is Olivia's fool and the jester replies that he is not: 'She will keep no fool, sir, till she be married' (lines 33–4). Rather, he is her 'corrupter of words' (line 37). The clown gives a good demonstration of his wit, his ability to make puns and Viola's appreciation (lines 61–9) complements Olivia's remark (Act I, Scene 5, lines 93–4): the clown's humour contains no 'slander'.

Feste treats Cesario with respect while at the same time demonstrating that he is equally witty. Cesario pays the clown who goes inside to announce his presence.

While waiting Cesario reflects on the role of the fool. To perform it well requires intelligence and sensitivity. The fool must be aware of the mood and social status of each person he makes fun of, measuring his wit to fit the occasion and not just let his jokes fly anywhere. To be a good fool, concludes Cesario, is as difficult as 'a wise man's art' (line 67).

At this point Sir Toby and Sir Andrew enter. The two knights are terribly impressed by Cesario's manners, and Sir Andrew in particular is struck by his courtly language: 'That youth's a rare courtier' (line 88) he observes. Later the knight's jealousy will be fuelled by this and give rise to the pretend duel between the two (Act III Scene 4).

When Olivia arrives she orders all the others to leave so that she can be alone with Cesario.

CHECKPOINT 15

Consider the way this scene continues the events of Act II Scene 4 in which Orsino sent Cesario to Olivia.

Olivia's response to Cesario reveals she is as changeable in love as Orsino.

Straightaway she asks for his hand. He keeps his distance, reminding her that he is her servant. As the servant of Orsino, who is her servant in love, he, Cesario, is therefore Olivia's servant.

Olivia is dismissive of such complicated reasoning. She wishes that Orsino thought nothing of her. She does not want to speak of the duke. She would much prefer it if Cesario had come to woo her for himself.

EXAMINER'S SECRET

If you are asked to write about this scene, make sure you present the two sides of the 'argument' clearly, using quotes from the speeches of both Olivia and Cesario.

She confesses that she sent Malvolio with the ring as an excuse to make him return to her. She is unhappy and wants Cesario to think well of her, even though she thinks he must despise her for being so honest about her feelings.

Cesario says he pities her. That at least is close to love, ventures Olivia. Cesario disagrees: we often pity our enemies, he says. Olivia cannot conceal her disappointment at being rejected by Cesario. She assures him that she will not pursue the subject further. Whoever marries Cesario will certainly be marrying a 'proper man' (line 135) she says.

As Cesario prepares to leave he asks Olivia one last time if she has any message for Duke Orsino. Olivia pleads with him to stay and tell her what he thinks of her.

CHECKPOINT 16

Why must Viola break all contact with Olivia?

The dialogue (lines 140–6) underlines the complications which the disguise has caused: both Cesario and Olivia are 'not what they are' – Cesario is really a woman; Olivia thinks she is in love with a man.

After some guarded and ambiguous dialogue in which both confess they are not what they appear to be, Olivia breaks into an impassioned declaration of her love for Cesario. No woman ever has or ever will conquer my heart, Cesario informs her, 'I have one heart, one bosom, and one truth' (line 160). Olivia begs him to come again in the hope that one day he may indeed be able to love her.

The final speeches of the scene are in **rhyming couplets** which distance us from the turbulent emotions being expressed and underline the artificiality and irony of the situation.

SCENE 2 – A trick played on Sir Andrew!

1. **Fabian tells Sir Andrew that Olivia is trying to make him jealous.**
2. **Sir Toby suggests that Sir Andrew challenge Cesario to a duel.**
3. **Maria reveals that Malvolio has taken to wearing yellow stockings.**

When writing about the subplot, don't forget to refer to the way it mirrors the action of the main plot.

The purpose of this short scene is chiefly to move the **subplot** along. Sir Toby and Fabian create some more comic mischief: this time at the expense of Sir Andrew.

Sir Andrew, Sir Toby and Fabian are in Olivia's house discussing Sir Andrew's attempt to win the affections of Olivia. Sir Andrew wants to give up and return to his home. He believes that Olivia cares more for the 'Count's serving-man' (line 5), Cesario, than she does for him. Sir Andrew has seen them together in the orchard. It was clear that Olivia was in love with the youth from the way she behaved.

CHECKPOINT 17

How do we learn more of Sir Andrew's stupidity?

Fabian tells him that she showed 'favour' (line 16) to Cesario just to make Sir Andrew jealous. What Olivia wanted was for Sir Andrew to march up to them and insult Cesario, and then he 'should have banged the youth into a dumbness' (line 21). As it is, the knight has lost a perfect opportunity to demonstrate his valour. He is therefore in her low opinion, where he must 'hang like an icicle on a Dutchman's beard' (lines 25–6) unless he redeems himself by some act of courage or strategy ('policy', line 28).

CHECKPOINT 18

How does Sir Andrew differ from Malvolio on the evidence of this scene?

Sir Andrew decides to do something courageous and Sir Toby suggests he challenge Cesario to a duel. He sends him off to write the challenge and gives him some advice on what to say.

When the foolish Aguecheek has gone, Sir Toby and Fabian laugh at this new practical joke they are playing. They are certain that neither Sir Andrew, who is a coward, nor Cesario, who is peaceable, will ever come to fight one another.

CHECKPOINT 19

This scene contains two references to important events in the 1500s. Can you locate them?

To complement this new practical joke we are given a glimpse of Malvolio's behaviour with Olivia, making two dupes. Maria arrives to inform them that Malvolio is obeying 'every point of the letter' (line 74). He has donned a pair of yellow stockings and 'does smile his face into more lines than is in the new map with the augmentation of the Indies' (lines 75–7). She leads them off the stage to enjoy the absurd result of their practical joke.

SCENE 3 – Loyal Antonio follows Sebastian

1. **Antonio tells Sebastian about his past.**
2. **Antonio lends Sebastian some money.**

Viola's twin brother, Sebastian, and Antonio the sea captain, walk in the street near Orsino's palace. The scene prepares us for the later complications of mistaken identity.

Antonio has done what he said he would do (Act II Scene 1) and followed Sebastian into Illyria. Antonio is shown as a brave and honest character. He tells Sebastian that he could not let him wander alone in a strange country: his affection and concern overcame any anxieties he had about his own safety: 'I could not stay behind you: my desire, / More sharp than filed steel, did spur me forth' (lines 4–5).

Antonio relates that he was once in a sea-fight against the duke's ships. He played such a prominent part in this battle that if he had been caught he would probably have been put to death.

Sebastian is full of gratitude for the risk Antonio has taken, and Antonio tells him that it would be best if he went undercover while Sebastian does some sightseeing. He hands Sebastian a purse containing money 'Haply your eye shall light upon some toy / You have desire to purchase' (lines 44–5). They agree to meet later at an inn called The Elephant. This gift of money will feature in the plot when Viola, disguised as Cesario, is mistaken by Antonio for Sebastian.

CHECKPOINT 20

There is a strong bond of friendship between the two men – look at Antonio's loyalty and concern, and Sebastian's gratitude. What dramatic purpose does this serve later in the play?

SCENE 4 – Malvolio's midsummer madness

1. **Olivia sends for Malvolio and he appears dressed in yellow stockings.**
2. **Olivia thinks Malvolio is mad and tells Maria to look after him.**
3. **Malvolio insults Sir Toby and his friends. Sir Toby plans to have him shut up in a dark room.**
4. **Sir Andrew produces the challenge he has written for Cesario. Sir Toby gives Sir Andrew some advice on how to fight Cesario.**
5. **Sir Toby warns Cesario that Sir Andrew wants to fight him.**
6. **Antonio appears and mistakes Cesario for Sebastian. He tries to protect him from Sir Andrew and offers to fight Sir Toby.**
7. **Orsino's officers arrest Antonio. Cesario denies that he knows Antonio but begins to believe Sebastian is alive.**

This scene is one of the two longest scenes in the entire play. It can be divided up into several sections featuring different groups of characters and exploiting the mistaken identities and deceptions

GLOSSARY

toy: trivial thing

which Shakespeare has been preparing in the previous scenes. The deceived or mistaken characters are Malvolio, Olivia, Viola, Sir Andrew and Antonio.

Olivia and Malvolio

CHECKPOINT 21

Note the part mistaken identity and deception play in this final scene of Act III and the way the different groupings of the characters are presented.

Olivia is in her garden expecting to entertain Cesario, whom she has invited to visit her. She wonders where Malvolio is. His serious and polite manner would soothe her disturbed emotions. Maria informs her that Malvolio is on his way to see her, but warns her mistress that he has become 'very strange' (line 8) and is probably possessed by the devil.

With a foolish smile on his face, Malvolio enters. Olivia is disconcerted. Her steward has shed his normally dark clothes and is wearing yellow stockings. He is far from the 'sad and civil' (line 5) Malvolio she is used to, having transformed himself into the ludicrous parody of a fawning courtier, smiling inanely and blowing her kisses, and making suggestive references to what he believes to be her feelings towards him.

He pays no attention to her expressions of surprise and confusion and continues to quote various lines from the forged letter. Olivia tries to get some sense out of him – what is this talk about 'greatness' (line 38)? – but Malvolio continues to ramble on, to such a degree of absurdity that Olivia concludes he is suffering from some kind of 'midsummer madness' (line 55).

The change in Malvolio's appearance is very dramatic and very funny. Much of the comedy is derived from his total confidence that Olivia knows what he is talking about when he quotes from the letter. Maria at this point is the only one on the stage who shares with the audience the truth of the joke. Malvolio has no idea he has been made to look such a fool.

The arrival of Cesario is announced and before she goes off to see him Olivia instructs Maria to take charge of the deranged Malvolio.

THE CHALLENGE

Left alone Malvolio recalls what the letter said concerning how he must treat Sir Toby ('be opposite with a kinsman', line 69) and when the knight enters, accompanied by Fabian and Maria, he is rude to them all. After he has left they plan to have him locked up in a dark room, the customary place for Elizabethan lunatics. Sir Toby reminds them that Olivia already thinks Malvolio is mad, so they can carry their joke a little further, 'for our pleasure, and his penance' (lines 138–9).

Another object of mockery enters, 'More matter for a May morning' (line 144). Sir Andrew Aguecheek is clutching the challenge he has just written to Cesario. He is very proud of this piece of writing and Sir Toby reads it out loud. The absurd language, full of wooden and obscure phrases, is ironically admired by Fabian. Sir Toby says he will personally deliver the challenge himself. Maria informs them that Cesario is at present with Olivia, so this would be an excellent time to hand it over.

Sir Toby advises Sir Andrew to approach Cesario from behind, with his sword drawn and swearing horribly. This will make the knight

DID YOU KNOW?

Malvolio has been identified as a possible caricature of Sir Christopher Hatton, who was Queen Elizabeth's steward and did, indeed, woo her. His manner was so fawning that some courtiers found him both hypocritical and ridiculous. The Queen called him her 'Sheep' or 'Mutton'.

CHECK THE FILM

Nigel Hawthorne, who plays Malvolio in Trevor Nunn's film of the play, says, 'He's a sad man, and in many ways completely ludicrous because he displays the height of conceit and pomposity'.

GLOSSARY

sad and civil serious and formal

More matter for a May morning another subject fit for a May pageant

Scene 4 continued

Of the 17,677 words that Shakespeare uses in his plays, sonnets and poems, his is the first use of over 1,700 of them!

look very tough and manly, far more than any actual deed of courage. Sir Andrew goes off to do battle with Cesario.

The manipulative aspects of Sir Toby's character are prominent in this scene. Aware that such an absurdly phrased challenge would not frighten the well-bred Cesario, but just make him think it came from an illiterate idiot, Sir Toby decides to deliver the challenge verbally. He will play off Aguecheek and Cesario against one another, making each so frightened 'that they will kill one another by the look, like cockatrices' (lines 196–7).

Olivia and Cesario

Just as the jokers are leaving the stage, Olivia enters with Cesario. Sir Toby decides to leave them together for a while to give him time to think up 'some horrid message for a challenge' (lines 201–2).

Olivia continues to woo Cesario. She gives him a jewelled brooch containing a miniature portrait of herself, and after telling him to return to her the next day, she leaves.

The duel

Sir Toby and Fabian then return. Sir Toby tells Cesario to prepare to defend himself, for his 'interceptor' (line 224), Sir Andrew, is waiting for him in the orchard. He must draw his sword quickly for Sir Andrew is a 'skillful, and deadly' (line 227) opponent.

Cesario can think of no man who might want to fight him; he has offended no one. Sir Toby paints a picture of Sir Andrew as a fearsome fighter, a 'devil' (line 238) who has killed three men already in disputes. Cesario becomes very alarmed and makes to return to Olivia's house to seek protection, but Sir Toby urges him on to fight – 'strip your sword stark naked' (line 254).

Cesario implores Sir Toby to go to this knight and discover what offence he has given and Sir Toby exits, pretending to do this, leaving the frightened courtier in the charge of Fabian. Fabian leads Cesario to 'the most skillful, bloody, and fatal opposite that you could possibly have found in any part of Illyria' (lines 270–2).

Sir Toby and Sir Andrew enter, and Aguecheek is soon reduced to terror by Sir Toby's description of Cesario's ferocity. He offers to give Cesario his horse 'Capilet' in order to pacify him, and when Cesario returns the two opponents are provoked to draw their swords. Their duel derives its comic irony from the fact that Olivia is unaware of Sir Andrew's intentions towards her and has been rejected by Cesario anyway.

Trouble for Antonio

Suddenly, Antonio enters. He sees Cesario and mistakenly believes it is his friend, Sebastian, Viola's twin brother. He calls on Sir Andrew to put up his sword, unless he wants to fight Antonio. Just as Sir Toby draws *his* sword and prepares to fight Antonio, a troop of officers arrive on the scene. They have come for Antonio. He has been recognised in the street and Orsino has sent them to arrest him.

DID YOU KNOW?

The unexpected entrance of Antonio points towards the uniting of Viola and Sebastian in Act V.

Antonio appeals to Cesario for help and asks him for the return of his money. Cesario, who at this point knows nothing of Antonio's mistake, denies he has been given any money by the man. But out of charity he offers to give him some money, since he has shown him such kindness.

Antonio is both grieved and angered by what he thinks is the ingratitude of a friend. Antonio is a decent, sincere man whose indignation is based on the fact of Viola's disguise – he feels he has been misled by Sebastian's appearance of nobility (**dramatic irony**). He tells the crowd that he once rescued this youth from 'the jaws of death' (line 369) and subsequently served him with great devotion. He turns on Cesario and curses him: 'But O how vile an idol proves this god! / Thou hast, Sebastian, done good feature shame' (lines 374–5). The officers take him away.

Antonio's entrance adds an additional absurdity to the scene. He attempts to defend 'Sebastian' (Viola disguised as Cesario) and ends up drawing swords with the pugnacious Sir Toby.

Hope for Viola

When Viola (Cesario) hears the name 'Sebastian' she becomes hopeful that Antonio's mistake reveals the possibility that her brother is still

GLOSSARY

cockatrices fabulous serpents that could kill with a glance

Scene 4 continued

alive. Surely, she thinks, it is possible that Antonio has indeed saved her brother from the shipwreck and because of her disguise has thought she was him: 'For him I imitate' (line 393). She leaves the stage.

DID YOU KNOW?

Shakespeare had a vocabulary of 30,000 words. Today, our vocabularies are between 6,000 and 15,000 words.

The end of the story is in sight

We sense at the end of the scene that the various elements of the plot's confusions are soon to be unravelled. Thus when Viola hears her brother's name it marks a turning point, even though the 'knot' will not be untied until after Sebastian has been mistaken for Cesario.

Sir Toby and Fabian squeeze out the last drop of fun from their joke by convincing the foolish Sir Andrew that Cesario is a coward and has run away. They urge him to follow the page and 'cuff him soundly' (line 401).

Now take a break!

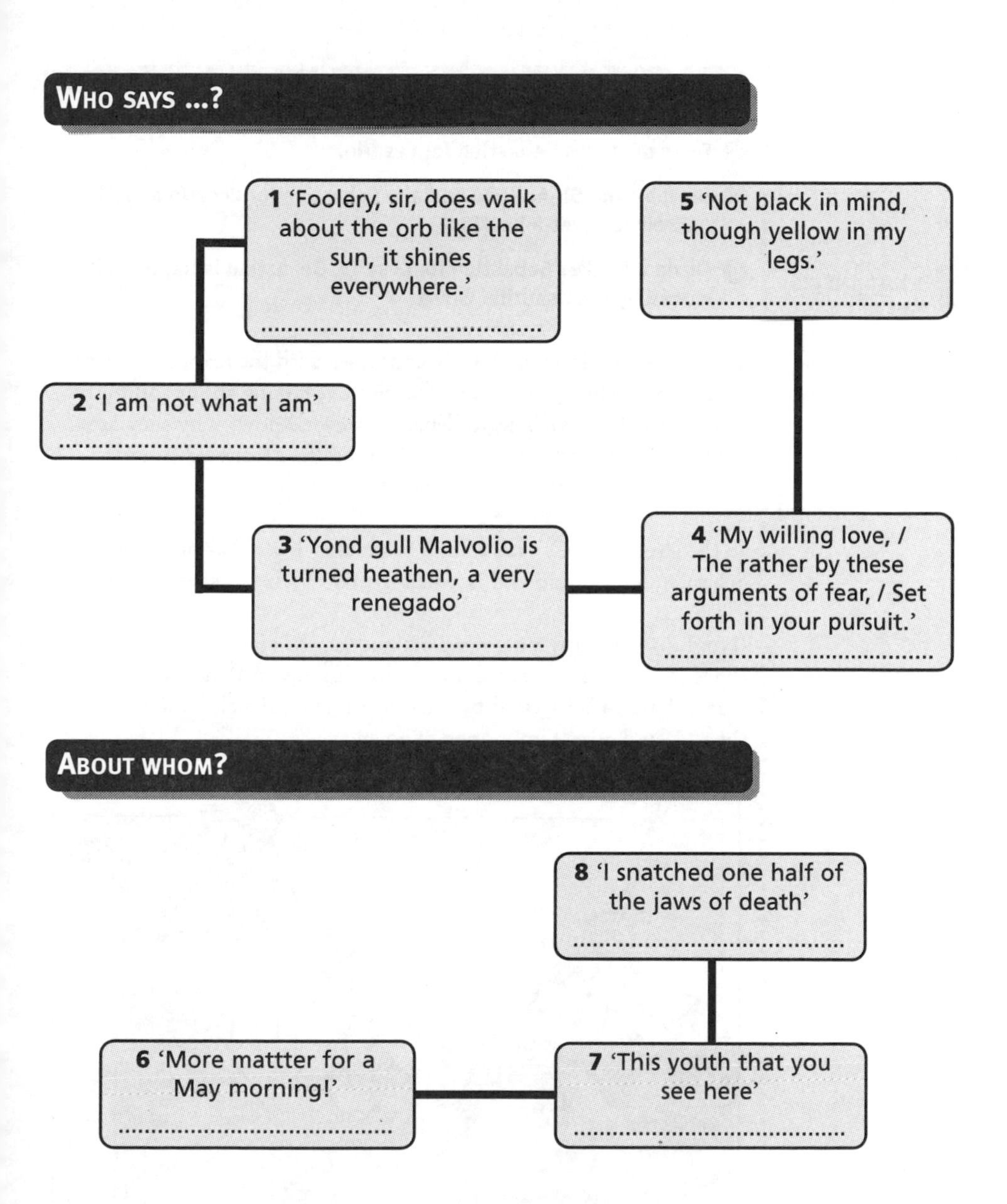

Check your answers on p. 97.

SCENE 1 – Sebastian lands in clover

1. **Feste mistakes Sebastian for Cesario.**
2. **Sir Toby and Sir Andrew mistake Sebastian for Cesario and Sir Andrew receives a beating.**
3. **Olivia mistakes Sebastian for Cesario. Sebastian is happy to be wooed by the beautiful Olivia.**

EXAMINER'S SECRET

To achieve at least a C grade, candidates need to have some insight into the relevance of a Shakespeare play.

The theme of mistaken identity continues with the reappearance of Sebastian. He does not know what Feste is talking about and Feste thinks he is Cesario. The audience, however, knows why they are confused – an excellent example of comically effective **dramatic irony** 'Nothing that is, is so' (lines 8–9).

In the street near Olivia's house, Feste, the clown, has mistaken Sebastian for Cesario and is insisting that Olivia has sent for him.

'No, I do not know you, nor I am not sent to you by my lady' (lines 5–6). Feste's lines are doubly ironical because they are in fact true. Sebastian is irritated by what he thinks is the clown's 'folly' (line 10) and gives him money to go away.

Sir Andrew, Sir Toby and Fabian enter. They too believe that Sebastian is Cesario and Sir Andrew strikes him. In return, Sebastian gives Sir Andrew a sound beating.

The comic results of a mistaken identity are taken further by Sir Andrew's reaction to Sebastian, whom he takes to be the 'coward' (V.I.179), Cesario.

Feste immediately goes off to report this to Olivia. Sir Toby decides to intervene and grabs hold of Sebastian. They draw their swords and are about to fight, when Olivia enters.

Olivia, also believing that Sebastian is Cesario, asks him to go into the house. She reprimands Sir Toby for his lack of manners and tells him to get out of her sight: 'Ungracious wretch, / Fit for the mountains and the barabarous caves, / Where manners ne'er were preach'd! Out of my sight! … Rudesby, be gone!' (lines 46–50).

When she is alone with Sebastian, Olivia apologises for her uncle's behaviour. She tells him that when he hears of the 'pranks' (line 54) Sir Toby has got up to in the past, he will smile. The wretched Sir Toby had made her afraid that someone dear to her heart was in danger, she confides. Sebastian is amazed at all this. He is being wooed by a beautiful woman whom he has never seen before. Is he mad? Or is he dreaming? 'Let fancy still my sense in Lethe steep; / If it be thus to dream, still let me sleep!' (lines 61–2).

Whichever is the case, he happily agrees to do whatever she asks.

A happy mistaking

The scene develops the turn of events which begin to resolve the problems and confusions of the main plot. Olivia believes that Cesario does indeed love her when Sebastian agrees to be 'rul'd' (line 63) by her: 'Madam, I will' (line 65). Obviously they are going to get married.

Shakespeare's formal education would have started at about the age of four or five with two years at 'petty school' where he was taught to read and write. At seven he would have started at the grammar school where the day began at 6 a.m. in the summer and lasted until 5 p.m. There were very few breaks or holidays.

GLOSSARY

fancy love
Lethe in classical mythology this was the river of oblivion in Hades

SCENE 2 – Sir Topas

1. **Feste dresses up as a priest, 'Sir Topas', and goes to torment Malvolio in the dark room.**
2. **Sir Toby wants to put an end to the trickery.**
3. **Feste goes to the dark room as himself and offers to take a message to Olivia for the unfortunate steward.**

Malvolio has been locked in a dark room to cure him of his 'midsummer madness' (III.4.55). Maria and Feste, the clown, enter and prepare one final trick on the puritanical steward.

As before, a disguise is used to create comedy. Feste dresses up as a priest, 'Sir Topas', who will interview Malvolio.

The colour of ignorance and humiliation

A parson's black gown is used here which is, ironically, the colour normally associated with Malvolio, who in contrast is dressed in bright colours. This reversal provides a visual symbol of just how thoroughly his pride has been humiliated.

When 'Sir Topas' talks to Malvolio he uses obscure Latin phrases and pseudo-philosophical arguments. The steward is relieved to hear a priest's voice and thinks he will soon be released. This does not happen: he will remain in 'darkness' (line 31) for some time. 'Sir Topas' leaves Malvolio crying for help.

Feste says 'there is no darkness but ignorance' (lines 43–4) and Malvolio's ignorance has been ruthlessly exposed in the scene. He was ignorant to think that Olivia could ever love him in the first place

Sir Toby, who has been brought back by Maria, tells the clown to assume his normal voice and speak to Malvolio. The knight wants to put an end to this 'knavery' (line 70) because he is out of favour with Olivia. He is worried that his niece will turn him out of the house. The scene's dramatic function is to let the **subplot** move towards its end. Sir Toby is keen to bring the joke to an end more out of self-interest than any concern for Malvolio.

CHECKPOINT 22

How does the fact that Sir Toby is out of favour with Olivia influence the comic **subplot** in Act IV Scene 2?

CHECKPOINT 23

Are we able to feel any sympathy for Malvolio at this point?

CHECKPOINT 24

What is the 'dark room' like? How would you make the scene appear sinister on stage?

CHECK THE BOOK

Compare this scene with a parallel scene in *The Comedy of Errors*.

Feste goes once more into the dark room, this time singing a popular song in his own voice. When Malvolio recognises him, he asks for 'a candle, and pen, ink, and paper' (line 84) so that he can send a message to Olivia.

In the darkness Feste makes Malvolio believe there are two people present by alternating his own voice with that of 'Sir Topas'. Malvolio asserts that he is not insane and that he has been 'notoriously abused' (line 90). This phrase will be repeated again with a touch of humour by Olivia at the end of Act V. 'Notoriously' is the kind of pretentious word Malvolio is fond of.

The clown goes off, singing, to fetch the writing materials.

DID YOU KNOW?

In Elizabethan England, people commonly attributed madness to possession by the devil. The 'cure' was often exorcism. Feste's exorcism of Malvolio, 'Out hyperbolical fiend! how vexest thou this man!' (lines 25–6), is comic only up to a point: how would you account for the rather sinister aspect to the scene?

SCENE 3 – Olivia takes Sebastian to the altar

1. **Sebastian considers his good fortune and wonders where Antonio has got to.**
2. **Olivia comes with a priest and they go off to be married.**

Sebastian sits alone in Olivia's garden reflecting on what has happened. Unexpectedly he is loved by a beautiful young countess who has given him a love token, a pearl; he can hardly believe his good fortune. 'This is the air, that is the glorious sun, / This pearl she gave me, I do feel't, and see't' (lines 1–2).

He wonders what has happened to Antonio. When he called at The Elephant he was told that Antonio was roving around the town looking for him. If only his trusted friend were here now, then he could perhaps give Sebastian some good advice.

Although he knows that he is not deluded, the circumstances are so strange that he is prepared to believe that either he or Olivia is mad. At least he recognises that 'There's something in't / That is deceivable' (lines 20–1).

Soon Olivia enters, accompanied by a priest. She asks Sebastian not to blame her for being in such a hurry, but she wishes him to go with

GLOSSARY

deceivable deceptive

her straightaway to her private chapel and marry her. The marriage will be kept secret until an appropriate time occurs for it to be made public. Sebastian agrees wholeheartedly and they exit.

CHECKPOINT 25

Think about how Shakespeare has developed the character of Sebastian throughout this Act.

Note that Olivia never addresses Sebastian as 'Cesario'. This would make it impossible for the audience to maintain belief in the marriage ceremony where naturally Cesario would have to be named. Shakespeare was not as concerned about these little points of realistic detail as a modern dramatist would be.

This is a **romantic comedy** and a happy ending, usually symbolised by a marriage, is called for. Sebastian questions the plausibility of it all, but accepts Olivia's invitation to the church without question. If we find ourselves denying that such an 'improbable fiction' (III.4.129) could take place, Shakespeare has anticipated our objections by incorporating this view in the dialogue. The **rhyming couplets** at the end (lines 132–5) reinforce the sense of artificiality and distance.

Now take a break! 

TEST YOURSELF (ACT IV)

WHO SAYS ...?

1 'Nothing that is so, is so.'

....

2 'Are all the people mad?'

....

3 'Madman, thou errest. I say there is no darkness but ignorance'

....

4 'I would we were well rid of this knavery.'

....

5 'Fool, there was never man so notoriously abused'

....

6 'This is the air, that is the glorious sun, / This pearl she gave me, I do feel't, and see't / And though 'tis wonder that enwraps me thus, / Yet 'tis not madness.'

....

7 'There's something in't / That is deceivable.'

....

ABOUT WHOM?

8 'Now sir, have I met you again? There's for you!'

....

9 'Nay, come, I prithee; would thou'dst be ruled by me!'

....

10 'Talkest thou nothing but of ladies'

....

Check your answers on p. 97.

SCENE 1 – Viola and Sebastian are reunited

1. **Antonio is brought before Orsino and mistakes Cesario for Sebastian.**
2. **Olivia accuses Cesario of failing to keep an appointment.**
3. **Orsino threatens to kill Cesario to spite Olivia.**
4. **Sir Andrew accuses Cesario of wounding him.**
5. **Sebastian appears and Cesario (Viola) recognises him as her twin brother.**
6. **Olivia discovers she has married Sebastian. Olivia calls for Malvolio's release. When he appears, the trick is explained.**
7. **Orsino promises to marry Viola.**
8. **Feste sings a final song.**

A feature of 'A'-grade writing on literature is the ability to see two possibilities of interpretations and to support a preference for one of them.

The single scene of the final Act provides a strong sense of completion because it is within this last scene that all the plots, mistakes and confusions have to be resolved. The dialogue alternates between verse and **prose**, reflecting the moods of the main plot and **subplot**

FESTE

Feste is on his way to deliver Malvolio's letter to Olivia. He is intercepted by Fabian who tries unsuccessfully to persuade the clown to let him see the letter. The duke enters with Cesario (Viola), Curio and some noble men. The clown entertains them and Duke Orsino is pleased by this – he gives Feste a gold coin and orders him to announce to Olivia that he has come to see her. The conversation in prose between Orsino and the clown establishes a light-hearted mood. Feste is carrying Malvolio's letter to Olivia which will later resolve the **subplot** of his gulling.

CHECKPOINT 26

Note how Shakespeare resolves the **subplot** and the main plot in this last scene.

ANTONIO AND 'SEBASTIAN'

While they are waiting Antonio is brought on by some officers. Cesario tells the duke that this is the man who intervened in his duel with Sir Andrew. Orsino recognises Antonio's face, even though the last time he saw it, it was 'besmear'd / As black as Vulcan, in the smoke of war' (lines 50–1). Antonio had been the captain of a tiny pirate ship which had fought against the most powerful of the duke's vessels.

Antonio protests that although he was at that time Orsino's enemy, he was never a pirate. He goes on to explain how he has come to be in Illyria. He points at Cesario who he still believes is Sebastian. He claims he has been bewitched by the 'ingrateful boy' (line 75) who is standing at Orsino's side. I rescued him from a shipwreck, he says, and cared for him with love and devotion for three months. In return, complains Antonio, he has denied he knows me and refused to give me back my money.

CHECKPOINT 27

How are the confusions caused by the various mistaken identities brought to a climax after the introduction of Antonio?

OLIVIA AND 'CESARIO'

Olivia enters with her attendants and Orsino immediately turns his attention to her, telling Antonio that Cesario has been his servant for the last three months and therefore Antonio's talk is 'madness' (line 96).

Olivia is annoyed. She asks Orsino what she can do for him and then accuses Cesario of failing to keep an appointment with her. Orsino becomes very angry with Olivia and his frustration makes him turn on Cesario, whom he knows Olivia loves. He threatens to kill him out of spite for Olivia. Cesario consents to follow Orsino and

GLOSSARY

Vulcan god of fire

submit to whatever fate he has in store for him, for he loves Orsino more than his life, 'More, by all mores, than e'er I shall love wife' (line 134). Olivia is horrified. She calls for the priest who married her to Cesario (in reality to Sebastian).

The priest enters and confirms that he did indeed marry them only two hours before. An enraged Orsino turns on Cesario and orders him to leave his sight forever. Cesario (Viola) tries to protest but is stopped by Olivia.

A FIGHT WITH 'CESARIO'

Shakespeare makes the audience wait a little longer for the resolution of these mistakes by bringing on Sir Andrew and Sir Toby, bruised and bleeding from their encounter with Sebastian. They in turn accuse the disguised Viola of assaulting them. Their description of 'Cesario' as a 'very devil incardinate' (line 179) makes a humorous contrast to the civilised and gentle Viola known to the audience.

Shakespeare must have been fully aware of the difference between idealised romantic love and the reality of marriage. He married at eighteen a woman eight years older than himself whom he had made pregnant. After two more children were born he left her behind in Stratford and went to London to make a name for himself.

Sir Andrew enters crying out for a surgeon. He and Sir Toby have been wounded by Cesario, he claims. Sir Andrew's head has been broken and Sir Toby has a 'bloody coxcomb' (line 174). Cesario (Viola) protests that he did not hurt Sir Andrew when the knight drew his sword, but merely spoke politely to him. Drunk and bleeding, Sir Toby comes on the scene with the clown, Feste, who tells him that the surgeon cannot attend because he is drunk. Sir Toby curses the surgeon: 'I hate a drunken rogue' (line 199), he says. Olivia soon puts a stop to all this 'havoc' (line 200) by sending Sir Toby off to bed and he departs while fighting off the unwanted attentions of Sir Andrew. The clown and Fabian follow them.

TWINS REUNITED

Sebastian, the cause of all this confusion, now enters. The appearance of Sebastian marks the resolution of all these mistakes, the recognition which the audience has been waiting for. When reading the play it is important to visualise this moment and imagine both twins dressed as men and therefore impossible for the other characters to tell apart.

Sebastian apologises to Olivia for injuring her uncle but explains that he would have had to do the same even if it had been his own brother, in order to protect himself. He notices that Olivia is looking at him strangely. He concludes she is very offended. Like Orsino and Antonio, Olivia is simply amazed at the extraordinary likeness between Sebastian and Cesario.

When Sebastian sees Cesario he too is astonished to see someone who looks so like himself – 'Do I stand there?' (line 224) – and asks him if they are related. Cesario (Viola) tells him that he looks very like a twin brother called Sebastian who drowned in a 'watery tomb' (line 232). Cesario's father was called 'Sebastian' also. Sebastian could be this brother's ghost.

As soon as Sebastian and Viola (Cesario) realise they had the same father, Viola reveals herself as Sebastian's lost sister. She says that she can confirm this by taking Sebastian to the sea captain who has been keeping her woman's clothes all this while, the same sea captain who helped her to disguise herself as 'Cesario' and serve the Duke Orsino as a messenger in his wooing of Olivia. Sebastian informs Olivia that she has been 'mistook' (line 257) and would have been married to a virgin girl if she had married 'Cesario' but since she in fact married him, Sebastian, she has married a virgin youth ('a maid and man' – line 261).

The Duke Orsino, going through another rapid change of emotion, turns to Viola and reminds her that, as 'Cesario', she had claimed many times that she would never love a woman as much as she loved him. He takes her hand and asks to see her dressed in her 'woman's weeds' (line 271). Viola replies that the captain who has her clothes is at present being kept in prison by Malvolio.

MALVOLIO IS ENLIGHTENED

Olivia calls for Malvolio so that the captain can be released. Feste returns carrying the steward's letter. Olivia orders the clown to read the letter out loud, but the affected voice he puts on is too distracting. She asks Fabian to read it. The duke does not believe a true madman could have written such a letter and Olivia tells Fabian to bring Malvolio before them.

CHECKPOINT 28

Make a note of all the different forms of 'recognition' that occur.

Shakespeare and his Comedies (1957) by John Russell Brown contains an excellent chapter on *Twelfth Night*.

GLOSSARY

bloody coxcomb bleeding head

woman's weeds woman's dress

PART THREE

COMMENTARY

THEMES

Twelfth Night is a **romantic comedy**, an Elizabethan style of play that Shakespeare developed with great success. Such a play usually concerns the love of an idealised couple who, after a series of misadventures and confusions, are finally united.

Disguised characters and a remote setting are also typical features of the romantic comedy (see also *As You Like It*).

However, although the play is termed a 'comedy', its themes are essentially serious, and Shakespeare uses the form to examine different aspects of human love, from its most absurd and deluded to its most authentic expression. In doing this he exploits to the full all the elements of the comic mode – as befits a play written for the festive season – from hilarious farce to sophisticated word-play.

DID YOU KNOW?

Twelfth Night was probably performed for the first time on February 2, 1602 at Middle Temple, an inn of court. 'A place away from [the Royal] court that had a well-established and thus protected tradition of giving plays ... that mocked government practices.' A safe haven for allowed fools!

LOVE

The play's opening lines sound its major theme, 'If music be the food of love, play on', and some form of love, real or imagined, dominates the emotions of all the main and some of the minor characters.

Firstly we are shown the idealised love of Orsino for Olivia whom he loves at a distance and through the messages he sends with Viola (Cesario). Such a lover is not dismayed by the fact that its object cannot respond; on the contrary, Orsino sees Olivia's decision to mourn her brother's death and live like a nun as proof of her 'sweet perfections' (I.1.39).

Orsino's love is self-regarding and egotistical; he sees himself as typical of all true lovers and refuses to accept rejection. He is prone to generalisations on the nature of love while unaware of how close he is to genuine feeling when he talks to Viola dressed as Cesario in Act II Scene 4.

Such deluded aspects of love are echoed in the love Olivia feels for Cesario. But here the deception is based on physical appearance. Olivia falls rapidly in love with 'this youth's perfections' (I.5.300) and yet fears that her 'eye' has misled her into love (I.5.313). The deluded lover is parodied in the **subplot** through the figure of Malvolio who believes unquestioningly that his beautiful mistress loves him.

Both Orsino and Malvolio are in different ways governed by the 'self-love' which Olivia accuses Malvolio of at the end of Act I Scene 5 (line 89) and the play's treatment of love seems to propose a distinction between love that is based on vanity or ambition, and love that is genuine and selfless. Viola's love for Orsino is an example of the latter. She endures with patience the 'barful strife' (I.4.41) of her situation, wooing another woman for the man she secretly loves, and only able to express her feelings indirectly. Another example of selfless love is in the loyalty and care with which Antonio treats Sebastian.

DID YOU KNOW?
There are five unrequited lovers in the play – three in the main plot (Orsino, Olivia and Viola) and two in the subplot (Sir Andrew and Malvolio).

DISGUISE

'Nothing that is so, is so' (IV.1.8–9)

DID YOU KNOW?
Although they took part in plays on the Continent, and participated in the **Commedia dell'arte**, women did not act on the English stage in Shakespeare's day. The parts of women, and sometimes of old men, were acted by child actors – boys whose voices had not yet changed.

Because women's parts were played by boy actors in Shakespeare's day, the original Elizabethan audience would have found a special sophistication in Viola's part: a boy dressing up as a woman who, in the play, disguises herself as a man. Viola's disguise, in fact, is central to the plot. It enables the audience to know more of the true situation when Olivia and Orsino are on stage. It is the cause of many of the dramatic complications and confusions which make up the story.

Many forms of disguise feature in the play:

- Emotions and intentions are disguised behind an outer appearance, a pretence, or an attitude. Olivia's pretence at mourning, for example, is quickly discarded when she meets Cesario.
- Orsino's love for Olivia can be seen as an elaborate pretence when it gives way to murderous anger in Act V, before he rapidly transfers his affections to Viola.
- Feste adopts a disguise to torment Malvolio in Act IV.

- Sir Toby Belch disguises his real motives behind his show of friendship for Sir Andrew Aguecheek.
- Even Malvolio's yellow stockings and cross garters are a kind of masquerade.

The dramatic **convention** of disguise produces uncertainties of meaning and emotion throughout the play. The lovers in *Twelfth Night* are at cross-purposes. They not only create comic misunderstandings but also challenge what we see in appearances, gender roles and platonic feelings for the same sex. With male actors playing women (one of whom, Viola, is disguised as a boy), the idea of a stable identity may seem as misleading as a disguise.

The play abounds in references to these different forms of disguise, to the gap between what appears to be true and what really is. Viola calls disguise 'a wickedness / Wherein the pregnant enemy does much' (II.2.26–7) when she realises that Olivia has fallen in love with her persona as Cesario. In the play's moral scheme, disguise or self-deception create frustration and confusion. Antonio, for example, in Act III Scene 4, regrets the 'devotion' which Sebastian's handsome features had inspired in him (lines 374–8). Ironically, though, he is mistaken; yet his comments on the nature of virtue are relevant to the play as a whole.

DID YOU KNOW?

Twelfth Night celebrations began in the fifth century when French and English churches created 'The Feast of Fools'. Temporary 'Bishops' and 'Archbishops of Fools' play-acted, revelled and created mischief.

Disguised characters were **stock characters** of comedy, but Shakespeare uses the device to give it wider significance. The play makes us consider what our beliefs about ourselves and others are based upon. The action of the play brings the true natures of Olivia, Orsino and Malvolio to the surface, and only Malvolio at the end seems unable to recognise himself, blinded as he is by pride and self-righteousness.

THE FESTIVE SPIRIT

The importance of pleasure, tolerance and generosity are emphasised in *Twelfth Night*, as befits a play written to be performed during the Christmas season. The 'Twelfth Night' festivities, held on 6 January, were celebrated by Queen Elizabeth and her court with a great banquet followed by an entertainment. If the play was written for such an occasion, then we have no difficulty accounting for its mixture of impossible romance, slapstick comedy and satire. These ingredients would have been the order of the day in a festival which descended from the ancient Roman 'Saturnalia' and the medieval 'Feast of Fools'.

The characters can be divided between those who have a straightforward commitment to pleasure and the 'good life', and those who don't.

The former group are led by Sir Toby, and his opening lines provide a clear statement of his philosophy: he deplores his young niece's vow to spend seven years in mourning – 'I am sure care's an enemy to life' (I.3.2–3). The melancholic atmosphere in Olivia's house contradicts the carefree values of Sir Toby. When Malvolio is sent to stop the carousing in Act II Scene 3 the conflict between pleasure and its denial is brought to a head.

'Dost thou think because thou art virtuous there shall be no more cakes and ale?' (II.3.114–15) – Sir Toby's blunt question to Malvolio sums up the anti-Puritan values which are shared by Feste, Sir Andrew and Maria. It is as much for this puritanism, as his conceit and arrogance, that Malvolio will be punished by the revellers.

DID YOU KNOW?

Shakespeare did not plan to publish his plays. In his day, there was no law protecting authors' copyright. Many printers got a hold of about half of his plays and printed them as their own.

A *carpe diem* theme runs through the play. This is the invitation to enjoy youth and life quickly, in the present, for it will soon pass.

CHECK THE BOOK

Read Marvell's 'To His Coy Mistress' (1681) and Robert Herrick's 'To the Virgins, to make much of Time' (1648) for examples of the *carpe diem* theme in poetry.

Feste's song (Act II Scene 3) expresses his plea: '*What is love? 'Tis not hereafter, / Present mirth hath present laughter: / What's to come is still unsure*' (lines 47–50). Both Olivia and Orsino are failing to 'seize the day' in their respective attitudes of nun and passive lover. In his role as commentator on the 'folly' of his superiors, Feste alludes to the fact that Olivia's sorrow will quickly pass: 'As there is no true cuckold but calamity, so beauty's a flower' (I.5.49–50). He is suggesting that Olivia's mourning is foolish and she that should be giving her young life to love.

Sebastian, Antonio, Viola and even finally Olivia, embody the values of generosity which are present in the play. Sebastian, in Act III Scene 3, is concerned to reward Antonio for his devotion – 'uncurrent pay' (mere thanks) (line 16) is not enough, he fears. And Antonio himself has displayed selfless giving in his loyalty to Sebastian, not least through providing him with money and protection in a strange land.

When Viola first meets Olivia she accuses her of keeping the gifts of beauty which nature has given her to herself: 'Lady, you are the cruell'st she alive / If you will lead these graces to the grave / And leave the world no copy' (I.5.244–6). Viola has a frank, loving nature. Her eloquent call to love in the scene arouses Olivia's feelings, even though ironically they are directed at 'Cesario'. Olivia speaks for the virtues of generous loving when she criticises Malvolio for his lack of a 'free disposition' (I.5.91) – his lack of magnanimity, and when, in Act III Scene 1, she tells Viola that 'Love sought is good, but given unsought is better' (line 158).

STRUCTURE

Although *Twelfth Night* can be divided into a main plot and a number of **subplots**, a useful way to approach its structure is to think first of the way different groups of characters are interwoven to make up a single texture.

1. Firstly, there are the aristocratic characters, Duke Orsino and the Countess Olivia, whose situation is given in the opening scene.
2. Then there are the shipwrecked twins, Viola and Sebastian, and their helpers, a sea captain and Antonio. The fate of these characters is the business of the main plot.
3. A third group is made up of the revellers, Sir Toby Belch, Sir Andrew Aguecheek, Maria, Fabian and Feste, the clown. Their actions constitute the subplots.
4. Between these groups moves the connecting figure of Feste, who clowns for Olivia and sings for Orsino, and who is part of the plan to gull Malvolio.
5. Outside all of this, Olivia's egotistical steward stands in isolation.

CONVENTIONS

Shakespeare took the love story of *Twelfth Night* from a short story called *The Historie of Apolonius and Silla* which in turn derives from an Italian play, *Gl'Ingannati* (1531). In *Twelfth Night* we find a number of **conventions** (disguise, gender confusion, twins) which are common to previous dramas being given fresh subtleties. For example, in the duel scene Viola's fear contains an element of realism which Shakespeare has introduced to an originally **stock situation** – as a woman she will have no knowledge of fighting.

Have a clear idea of how the characters are grouped. This will make the story easier to understand and write about.

The standard Elizabethan five-act form allows Shakespeare to develop, scene by scene, alternating aspects of each of the plots:

- Acts I and II are an exposition in which all the basic situations are set up.
- Act III moves towards a climax, the appearance of Malvolio in yellow stockings and cross garters.
- The three short scenes of Act IV prepare the resolution of all the complications.
- This takes place in the long single scene of Act V.

Within this framework Shakespeare controls the audience's response and expectations with considerable skill. By the end of Act I, four situations have been given which provide the impetus for the rest of the play:

1. Orsino's unrequited love for Olivia
2. Sir Toby's unruly behaviour in Olivia's house and his self-interested friendship with the rich Sir Andrew Aguecheek
3. Viola's disguised love for Orsino
4. Olivia's love for Cesario

All these situations are potentially disastrous (imagine the same predicaments treated in the tragic mode), yet *Twelfth Night* is a comedy and the audience expects a happy ending. The plot of a comedy always takes the main characters from failure to success.

Shakespeare signals the possibility of such an ending by introducing Sebastian at the start of Act II: we know he is going to play an important part in the solution to the 'problem' because he goes off to Orsino's court. To emphasise the 'problem', Shakespeare allows Viola an opportunity to express it in her **soliloquy** at the end of Act II Scene 2 (lines 16–40). Like Viola, the audience is made to expect 'time' (i.e. the action of the play) to unravel the 'knot' (II.2.39–40).

SUBPLOTS

CHECK THE BOOK

Subplots are a very common feature of Elizabethan and Jacobean drama. Read Shakespeare's *King Lear* where the subplot of Gloucester and his two sons reflects the plight of Lear and his daughters.

The chief **subplot**, the gulling of Malvolio, provides a parallel and comic contrast to the more serious plot featuring the aristocratic figures of Orsino and Olivia, Viola and Sebastian.

It gets properly underway in Act II Scene 3, after Malvolio interrupts the drinking party. Shakespeare has carefully prepared the audience's response to this by depicting Malvolio in previous scenes as an increasingly unsympathetic figure. This occurs through his own words and actions, and through the words of other characters (e.g. Act I Scene 5 and Act II Scene 2).

Another subplot, also featuring Sir Toby and his friends, is interlocked with the gulling of Malvolio: Sir Andrew Aguecheek's foolish belief that he could marry Olivia. This is taken up in Act III. Both subplots feature an absurd letter and an absurd suitor for Olivia.

The play has a logical structure developing from what we already know, raising expectations and providing surprising incidents.

In the structure of *Twelfth Night* the actions that anticipate future events and raise audience expectations can be summarised as follows:

- Viola's assumption of a disguise (Act I Scene 2)
- Sir Toby persuades Sir Andrew to stay and woo Olivia (Act I Scene 3)
- The appearance of Sebastian (Act II Scene 1)
- Viola's soliloquy (Act II Scene 2)
- Malvolio's behaviour (Act I Scene 5 and Act II Scene 2)
- When Sir Toby and Sir Andrew meet 'Cesario' (Act III Scene 1)
- When Antonio gives Sebastian money (Act III Scene 3)
- When Antonio calls Cesario (Viola) 'Sebastian' (Act III Scene 4)

CHARACTERS

ORSINO

Duke Orsino's opening speech in Act I tells us something about his character and mood; he is in love, but this does not bring him happiness, rather a profound melancholy. His speech turns to images of disease and death – 'excess … surfeiting … sicken … die … dying' (lines 2–4) – and it is clear that Orsino is not an active lover focused on his beloved. He is preoccupied with the sensation of love itself, feeding his emotions with music and elaborate poetic imagery. Orsino has probably seen Olivia only once, and her image has inspired in him a kind of romantic indulgence, a belief that if she does not love him in return, he will die. From this passive, self-regarding emotion comes his employment of Cesario (Viola) as a messenger who will do his wooing for him.

Melancholic
In love with love
Eloquent and poetic
Inconsistent
Attractive

Orsino is an inconsistent character as Feste points out in Act II Scene 4, with a mind of 'opal' (line 75). He begs for music to reflect his mood, then quickly becomes bored. This changeable nature, however, makes believable his sudden transference of affection from Olivia to Viola at the end of the play. Perhaps his sudden outburst of anger in the final scene also indicates repressed aspects of his character.

However, if Viola is to fall in love with Orsino, then his character must justify this to the audience. He is described by Olivia in Act I Scene 5 as 'virtuous … noble …' (line 262), a wealthy, well-educated, courteous and handsome man. These are the qualities that make Viola fall in love with him.

VIOLA

Resourceful
Accomplished
Intelligent
Honest
Depth of feeling

Viola stands between the two extremes of emotion represented by Orsino and Olivia and as such she embodies a kind of norm of behaviour in the heady atmosphere of Illyria.

From our first encounter with her in Act I we learn that she is a practical person who makes the best of her situation as a shipwrecked orphan, and a woman in a strange land. Her decision to disguise herself as a eunuch denotes both courage and resourcefulness. She is trusting enough to take the sea captain's help and resolves to use her accomplishments to gain employment in Orsino's court.

Viola reveals her intelligence, wit and charm throughout the play, qualities that enable her to gain Orsino's special confidence and that cause Olivia to fall in love with her at first sight.

Her conversations with Orsino and Olivia show that she is an honest straightforward character in spite of the deception she is forced to enact for her own survival. She loyally continues to try to win Olivia's love for Orsino, even though she loves him herself.

Viola treats Olivia with dignity when the countess has confessed her love for her (as Cesario). Her capacity for deep feeling is clear from the story she tells Orsino in Act II Scene 4: 'My father had a daughter lov'd a man …' (lines 108–16).

OLIVIA

We learn a good deal about Olivia before she actually appears on the stage in the last scene of Act I. Her beauty is the cause of Orsino's poetic love in the first scene; in Scene 2 the captain tells Viola about the 'virtuous maid' (line 36) who had been orphaned and lost a brother; the third scene is set in her house; she is the subject of the conversation between Orsino and Cesario in Scene 4. She is therefore a character much anticipated by the audience by the time she finally appears.

Virtuous
Melancholic
Intelligent
Impetuous
Compassionate

On the face of it, Olivia's melancholy, her extravagant vow to mourn her brother for seven years, counterbalances the excessive romantic melancholy of Orsino. She is thus capable of self-deception, as the play subsequently demonstrates.

But Olivia has other, more attractive qualities. She is seen as intelligent and adaptable in her dealings with other members of her household – she soon allows Feste to win her over with his clowning, and her characterisation of Malvolio is cogent (Act I Scene 5). And her response to Malvolio's humiliation reveals a compassionate nature.

The quality that most characterises Olivia, however, is her capacity for impetuous feeling. She pursues Cesario relentlessly, with little concern for the decorum demanded by her own status as a countess and 'his' as a servant. Although she is able to rationalise Orsino's attractive qualities, she has no difficulty rejecting him as a lover. The comic irony of her situation lies partly in this irrational pursuit of Cesario.

Like Orsino, her feelings at the end are quickly transferred from one object of love to another.

SIR TOBY BELCH

Carefree
Irresponsible
Witty
Manipulative
Self-interested

Olivia's uncle is a large, earthy and jolly knight who is devoted to pleasures of the flesh, as his name suggests and as his behaviour throughout the play indicates. He is also a keen-witted person, even when he is drunk, and his intelligence contrasts sharply with his dupe, Sir Andrew Aguecheek.

In his relationship with Sir Andrew, Sir Toby displays a manipulative side to his character. He fools the gullible knight into believing that he could marry Olivia so that he will remain in her house and continue to finance Sir Toby's drinking habit. He loves a practical joke, especially when it is ingenious, and for her ability to think up such a clever trick as the gulling of Malvolio, he marries Maria.

In spite of his carefree and irresponsible nature, there is something of the bully in Sir Toby. He makes fun of Sir Andrew and Malvolio only as far as his self-interest allows: when there is a real possibility that Olivia will throw him out of the house, he loses interest in the two gulls.

MALVOLIO

Puritanical
Self-important
Humourless
Vain
Self-deluded

Malvolio is Olivia's steward and an important member of her household. But he is not as important as he would like to be. He is socially inferior to Sir Toby and deeply resents the irresponsible knight's riotous behaviour.

Malvolio is always serious and he has absolutely no sense of humour. He believes in dignity, good manners and order. He is always dressed in black.

In the play Malvolio is revealed as a hypocrite and an egotist. Beneath the puritanical exterior resides a vain, intolerant, ambitious personality whose conceit makes him an easy target for the practical jokers.

At the end of the play Malvolio is excluded from the general happiness and good fortune of the other main characters. He is incapable of self-knowledge.

SIR ANDREW AGUECHEEK

A tall, thin and very stupid knight. He is staying in Olivia's house at the invitation of Sir Toby Belch. He is rich, and Sir Toby encourages him to continue wooing the inaccessible countess so that he will finance their regular drinking sessions.

MARIA

Olivia's waiting-gentlewoman. She is sharp-witted, practical and inventive; she devises and manages the trick that is played on Malvolio. She eventually marries Sir Toby.

FESTE

A clown employed by the Countess Olivia. His role in the play is to provide music and witty comment. His foolery is everywhere, since he moves freely between the households of both Olivia and Orsino. This and his critical attitude towards the other characters makes him appear a rather detached character. He is very good at his job (as Viola recognises in III.1.60) and is paid for his wit on several occasions in the course of the play.

Apart from singing and providing verbal repartee, he is enrolled to participate in slapstick comedy when he dresses as 'Sir Topas'. Feste represents the festive spirit of the play, but there is also something touchy and cynical about him.

SEBASTIAN

Viola's twin brother who she becomes separated from after the shipwreck. Like his sister, he is helped by a sea captain (Antonio) to make his way to Illyria. He is mistaken for Cesario and marries Olivia.

A handsome, modest and courageous man, Sebastian is rather more emotional than his sister (Viola) and grieves deeply when he thinks she has drowned in the shipwreck. He appreciated Antonio's loyalty but does not want to cause him any misfortune.

As the masculine counterpart to Viola (Cesario) he becomes Olivia's 'natural' husband.

ANTONIO

A sea captain who rescues and befriends Sebastian. He risks his life to follow Sebastian and is arrested by Orsino's officers.

There was no Arts Council in Shakespeare's day. Soon after he arrived in London he dedicated two long and brilliant poems to Henry Wriothesley, Earl of Southampton, and in return received financial support.

FABIAN

A servant of Olivia's. He participates in the gulling of Malvolio and later assists Sir Toby in the trick that is played on Sir Andrew and Cesario.

VALENTINE AND CURIO

Two gentlemen attending on the Duke Orsino.

A SEA CAPTAIN

The captain of the wrecked ship who helps Viola with her disguise. He appears only once in the play.

LANGUAGE AND STYLE

CHECK THE BOOK

Shakespeare's Imagery and What It Tells Us by Caroline Spurgeon (1968) is an interesting study of language patterns and themes in Shakespeare's plays.

In Shakespeare's plays the language is of great importance. The Elizabethan actors were expected to deliver their lines with an emphasis on the expressive power of the words. The representation of character through, for example, gesture or facial expression was secondary to this. Therefore, in a way, the flow of language is where the action is; like a musical score it forms a complex pattern of sound and meaning.

Shakespeare basically uses three styles of writing in his dialogue: **poetic verse**, **blank verse** and **prose**. We will look at examples of all three and then you should find others as you read and study the play.

1 POETIC VERSE

'Enough, no more;
'Tis not so sweet now as it was before.
O spirit of love, how quick and fresh art thou,
That notwithstanding thy capacity
Receiveth as the sea, nought enters there,
Of what validity and pitch soe'er,
But falls into abatement and low price,
Even in a minute! So full of shapes is fancy,
That it alone is high fantastical.' (I.1.7–15)

Here Orsino is revealing his inner emotional state in language that is both 'poetic' and psychologically realistic. The rhyming words, e.g. 'more ... before' indicate his rather literary, formal expression of love. Note also the **alliterations** in 'capacity ... receiveth ... sea'. The **diction** is mostly made up of abstract words, 'spirit of love ... capacity ... validity ... pitch'. The **simile** of the vast sea indicates the vague and generalising aspect of his temperament (see Feste's comment on Orsino i.e. II.4.75–9).

The basis of this kind of poetic language is the comparison At its simplest, you can compare something directly with something else: '...you will hang like an icicle on a Dutchman's beard' says Fabian (in prose) to Sir Andrew in Act III Scene 2 lines 25–6. This sort of direct comparison is known as a **simile**.

A more subtle form of comparison is the **metaphor**. There are numerous examples but Viola uses it particularly effectively when, to the captain, she describes the way outwardly beautiful people can be bad inside: '...that nature with a beauteous wall / Doth oft close in pollution' (I.2.48–9).

Similes and **metaphors** form part of the play's imagery. The references to seas, waves, tempests, drowning, or the many references to music, appearance and truth affect the audience's imaginative responses. Once you start to be aware of these patterns of language you will be able to make connections between different themes.

2 BLANK VERSE

Blank verse was first used in the middle of the sixteenth century. Much of the finest poetry – by Shakespeare, Milton, Tennyson and Wordsworth – has been in this form. It can also be found in European literature.

Blank verse is the basic form of dramatic verse used by Shakespeare. It has the same rhythm or metre of five **iambs** and is close to the stresses of spoken English. It is very flexible and long sentences can be built up into **verse paragraphs**. Technically, blank verse consists of unrhymed **iambic pentameters**: in other words a line with ten syllables, five of which are stressed as indicated in this speech:

DID YOU KNOW?

A major item on the curriculum of Shakespeare's grammar school would have been the art of persuasion (rhetoric). It's almost certain he would have encountered *De Copia* (1512), a textbook by Erasmus on how to cultivate 'copiousness', verbal richness. It contains 144 ways of saying 'Thank you for your letter'!

EXAMINER'S SECRET

Never go through a text just listing all the figures of speech without explaining their effect and purpose.

'Well, gránt it thén,
And téll me, ín the módestý of hónour,
Why yóu have gíven me súch clear líghts of fávour,
Bade mé come smíling ánd cross-gárter'd tó you,
To pút on yéllow stóckings, ánd to frówn
Upón Sir Tóby, ánd the líghter péople' (V.1.333–8)

This is the only time in the play that Malvolio speaks in blank verse. Notice the way the lines have an argumentative tone and the feel of normal conversational English in the build up of the clauses. The **metaphor,** 'clear lights', recalls Malvolio's exclamation 'Daylight and champaign discovers not more!' (II.5.160), after he read the forged letter.

Shakespeare also uses the blank verse rhythm – the **iambic pentameter** – with rhyme. When the rhymes are paired, they are known as **rhyming couplets**. In his earlier plays, Shakespeare used a higher percentage of rhymed lines in his plays. As he grew older, he seems to have realised that blank verse was far more flexible.

In *Twelfth Night* one place where the **rhymed couplet** is used with some dramatic effect is at the end of Act III Scene 1 beginning at line 149. Olivia and Viola have had a very tense conversation in which Viola has come close to admitting who she really is: 'I am not what I am' (line 143). Olivia declares her love for 'Cesario' in a rhymed speech: 'I love thee so that maugre all my pride, / Nor wit nor reason can my passion hide' (lines 153–4). When Viola replies she takes up this rhyming pattern – 'By innocence I swear, and by my youth, / I have one heart, one bosom, and one truth,' (lines 159–60) – and this has the effect of underlining the artificial situation as well as neatly rounding off the action of the scene.

Another use of the rhymed couplet at the end of a scene might be to warn the actors waiting in the wings that it is time to enter.

When writing about speeches in the play look at the way punctuation marks are used. You will see lines that are not **end-stopped,** that is, there is no punctuation mark at the end. This breaks up the rhythm of blank verse (the five 'beats'). This is known as **enjambement**

Sometimes the sentence begins or ends in the middle of a line. This also breaks up the rhythm and can reinforces the idea of a person struggling to come to terms with ideas. Look at Malvolio's 'Well, grant it then' in the above example: he simply finds it impossible to believe that Olivia could have had anything to do with his humiliation, while at the same time he is clinging to his belief in the delusion that she really did write the letter. It may come as a surprise but there is a name for this deliberate breaking of a line of poetry, **caesura**.

3 PROSE

Prose is most often given to minor or comic characters in the play. About half the dialogue in *Twelfth Night* is in prose. Sometimes it is used to develop the plot or provide important information about a character or an event; for example, when Olivia characterises Malvolio in Act I Scene 5, she speaks in prose which is memorable for its eloquent perception of his character. 'O, you are sick of self-love, Malvolio, and taste with a distempered appetite …' (I.5.89–90).

EXAMINER'S SECRET

Always focus on the language of the text in your essays. Know the key quotations from each important scene and practise using them.

When Fabian is leading on Sir Andrew Aguecheek in Act III the prose seems very appropriate for the rich irony of Fabian's mockery:

> 'She did show favour to the youth in your sight only to exasperate you, to awake your dormouse valour, to put fire in your heart, and brimstone in your liver. You should then have accosted her, and with some excellent jests, fire-new from the mint, you should have banged the youth into dumbness'. (III.2.16–22)

Fabian's speech has a rhetorical verve and humour which is irresistible. 'Brimstone in your liver' parallels 'fire in your heart' in a way that shows Shakespeare's genius for the unusual and vivid image. Although the tone is more informal and straightforward than verse, the language still contains a **metaphorical** brilliance.

LINGUISTIC DEVICES

One final point on the language of the play is that Shakespeare employs a wide variety of linguistic devices. The language at times

An A-grade student is able to provide a detailed account of language features, or structured patterns, to support a conclusion about the author's intentions.

seems rather overloaded with **puns, antitheses, paradoxes** and **oxymoron**. Many of these he would have acquired from his training in rhetoric at the grammar school in Stratford. But his mind seems to have been very receptive to language drawn from all aspects of life, not merely academic book learning. Consequently he was able to make connections and comparisons in surprising and creative ways in order to illuminate his subject. The lines of Malvolio's grinning face are likened to a new map of the East Indies (Act III, Scene 3, lines 75–7); Viola describes, indirectly, the psychological effect of her suppressed feelings for Orsino as 'like a worm i'the bud / Feeds on her damask cheek' (I.4.112–113); and Fabian mocks Sir Andrew's challenge with a nautical metaphor: 'Still you can keep to the windy side of the law …' (III.4.165).

Shakespeare, like Feste and Sir Toby Belch, must have enjoyed playing around with words, even when it seems inappropriate!

Now take a break! 

PART FOUR

RESOURCES

HOW TO USE QUOTATIONS

One of the secrets of success in writing essays is the way you use quotations. There are five basic principles:

1. Put inverted commas at the beginning and end of the quotation.
2. Write the quotation exactly as it appears in the original.
3. Do not use a quotation that repeats what you have just written.
4. Use the quotation so that it fits into your sentence.
5. Keep the quotation as short as possible.

Quotations should be used to develop the line of thought in your essays. Your comment should not duplicate what is in your quotation. For example:

> **Viola (in Act II Scene 2 of *Twelfth Night*) tells us that she thinks disguises are wicked, 'Disguise, I see thou art a wickedness'** (line 26).

Far more effective is to write:

> **Viola describes disguise as 'a wickedness'** (II.2.26).

Always lay out the lines as they appear in the text. For example:

> **Viola answers Orsino's question with a riddle: 'I am all the daughters of my father's house, /And all the brothers too: and yet I know not'** (II.4.121–2).

or:

> **'I am all the daughters of my father's house**
> **And all the brothers too: and yet I know not'** (II.4.121–2).

However, the most sophisticated way of using the writer's words is to embed them into your sentence:

CHECK THE NET
http://shakespeare.palomar.edu/bestsites.htm and: **http://web.uvic.ca/shakespeare/Library/SLTnoframes/intro/introsubj.html** are excellent web sites on Shakespeare.

DID YOU KNOW?

One of Shakespeare's favourite writers was probably a Frenchman called Montaigne. He only wrote essays!

It is really Malvolio's 'self-love' (I.5.89) which makes him easy to trick.

When you use quotations in this way, you are demonstating the ability to use text as evidence to support your ideas – not imply including words from the original to prove you have read it.

COURSEWORK ESSAY

Set aside an hour or so at the start of your work to plan what you have to do.

- List all the points you feel are needed to cover the task. Collect page references of information and quotations that will support what you have to say. A helpful tool is the highlighter pen: this saves painstaking copying and enables you to target precisely what you want to use.
- Focus on what you consider to be the main points of the essay. Try to sum up your argument in a single sentence, which could be the closing sentence of your essay. Depending on the essay title, it could be a statement about a character: Viola is a witty, charming and loyal character because she wins Orsino's trust within only three days; an opinion about setting: Shakespeare set *Twelfth Night* in a far away place to emphasise the mood of romance and unreality; or a judgement on a theme: I think that the main theme of *Twelfth Night* is love, because most of the characters in the play experience this emotion.
- Make a short essay plan. Use the first paragraph to introduce the argument you wish to make. In the following paragraphs develop this argument with details, examples and other possible points of view. Sum up your argument in the last paragraph. Check you have answered the question.
- Write the essay, remembering all the time the central point you are making.
- On completion, go back over what you have written to eliminate careless errors and improve expression. Read it aloud to yourself, or, if you are feeling more confident, to relative or friend.

If you can, try to type you essay, using a word processor. This will allow you to correct and improve your writing without spoiling its appearance.

SITTING THE EXAMINATION

Examination papers are carefully designed to give you the opportunity to do your best. Follow these handy hints for exam success:

BEFORE YOU START

- Make sure you know the subject of the examination so that you are properly prepared and equipped.
- You need to be comfortable and free from distractions. Inform the invigilator if anything is off-putting, e.g. a shaky desk.
- Read the instructions, or rubric, on the front of the examination paper. You should know by now what you have to do but check to reassure yourself.
- Observe the time allocation – and follow it carefully. If they recommend 60 minutes for Question 1 and 30 minutes for Question 2, it is because Question 1 carries twice as many marks.
- Consider the mark allocation. You should write a longer response for 4 marks than for 2 marks.

EXAMINER'S SECRET

Higher-level achievement begins at the point when you show you are aware that you are being marked.

WRITING YOUR RESPONSES

- Use the questions to structure your response, e.g. question: 'The endings of X's poems are always particularly significant. Explain their importance with reference to two poems.' The first part of your answer will describe the ending of the first poem; the second part will look at the ending of the second poem; the third part will be an explanation of the significance of the two endings.
- Write a brief draft outline of your response.
- A typical 30-minute examination essay is probably between 400 and 600 words in length.

- Keep your writing legible and easy to read, using paragraphs to show the structure of your answers.
- Spend a couple of minutes afterwards quickly checking for obvious errors.

WHEN YOU HAVE FINISHED

- Don't be downhearted – if you found the examination difficult, it is probably because you really worked at the questions. Let's face it, they are not meant to be easy!
- Don't pay too much attention to what your friends have to say about the paper. Everyone's experience is different and no two people ever give the same answers.

Shakespeare did not write essays!

IMPROVE YOUR GRADE

Your potential grades in any examination can be improved. An examiner marks your work according to a mark scheme that is applied to all candidates and no examiner knows in advance your level of achievement. Thus every candidate everywhere starts at the same point: a blank answer booklet.

The exam board has determined that your answer booklet has more than enough space in it for you to get the highest marks so there's no need to rush your writing to fill up three or four extra sheets! Moreover, the two hours your examination is scheduled to last will be enough for a candidate to secure the highest marks without rushing.

So take your time. Think carefully, plan carefully, write carefully and check carefully. A relaxed performer always works best – in any field and in every examination! Whatever you are studying, the way to be completely at ease with it in an examination is to know it inside out. There is no substitute for reading and re-reading the text.

DID YOU KNOW?
Always have a spare pen!

Twelfth Night is conveniently divided into five Acts and in your study strategy you should make use of these divisions. Using a single sheet for each Act and list what happens in the story. This enables you to be familiar with the precise sequence of events.

Do the same for characters, devoting a single sheet to each of them. On this you should identify who they are, what they do and what they say. Back up the notes with short relevant quotations. These can be used to build up a character study or to support comments you wish to make in an essay.

You may be allowed to take the text into the examination hall but reference to it may well cost you valuable time unless you know it thoroughly. Your revision notes on plot and character are the ideal last-minute revision aids. You will almost certainly know more than enough to secure a high grade; the important thing is to make the most of what you have learnt.

The main reason why candidates let themselves down in the examination room is that they fail *to read the question!* Do not begin writing until you are quite sure what you want to say because it is very easy to lose track and end up writing off the subject. Whilst you are writing, it is a good idea to check back occasionally to the question and satisfy yourself that you are still answering it.

Keep an eye on the clock. Most literature papers require you to answer two questions in two hours. It may seem obvious but it is worth reminding yourself that to do yourself justice you need to spend about an hour on each question! This is all the more important when you feel happier answering one question rather than the other. If you steal time to produce a lengthy answer on one question, you are far more likely to lose all the extra marks you have gained by handing in a feeble response for the question you did not like.

Watch the clock and divide your time evenly between the answers.

Let's consider how you could approach the following question:

Describe the different kinds of love in the play.

BRAINSTORM THE QUESTION:

- Restate and define how you interpret key words in the question with synonyms or in your own words.
- Use these equivalent terms throughout your answer to keep focused.

- Write down everything you can think of that is connected to the question.
- Think of specific sentences that could be used to start the first paragraph.

You must first of all identify the kinds of love to be found in the play:

- The deluded 'romantic' love of Orsino for Olivia
- The true romantic love felt by Viola for Orsino
- The parodies of love shown in the characters of Sir Andrew and Malvolio
- The self-love of Malvolio and to some extent Orsino
- The love of life and the senses shown in the character of Sir Toby Belch
- The pure love of Viola for Sebastian
- The platonic love felt by Antonio for Sebastian

Improving your response from a D to a C

EXAMINER'S SECRET

Plan your answer using a spider graph or paragraph plan. Cross it through before handing in your paper.

- Instead of writing **'there are lots of examples of love in *Twelfth Night*'** write **'in *Twelfth Night* the romantic love felt by Orsino for Olivia is contrasted to the ridiculous love felt by Sir Andrew and Malvolio'**. The first statement is a loose generalisation but the second makes specific distinctions.
- Instead of stringing together a list of quotations that describe love, focus on the characters' reactions to the emotion. For example, **'Orsino describes love as "full of shapes" and "high fantastical" which reflects his rather abstract attitude to it'**.
- Instead of pointing out a few features relevant to the question, provide a more sustained response to specific situations, ideas or the author's purposes. This means writing in fully developed paragraphs!

IMPROVING YOUR RESPONSE FROM A C TO A B

A 'B' candidate begins to develop and explore his/her response with a range of examples:

- Instead of writing **'Viola secretly loves Orsino and the audience knows this'** write **'The fact that the audience already knows that Viola is really a man, and that Olivia is completely unaware of this, gives the situation both humour and sadness'.**
- Instead of putting in a couple of quotations, use a range of short quotations to illustrate your points. For example, **'Even though Orsino is** "virtuous", "noble", "of great estate" **and** "gracious", **Olivia cannot love him'.**
- Instead of picking out metaphors and similes, show how they might affect the audience's response: **'Fabian's metaphor for a jest,** "fire-new from the mint" **(III.2.16–22), would strike the audience as particularly funny, since Sir Andrew has shown himself to be useless with language'.**

EXAMINER'S SECRET

If your question contains bullet points covering topics relevant to the answer, use them to help structure your response.

IMPROVING YOUR RESPONSE FROM A B TO AN A

A feature of 'A' standard writing is insight, namely a shrewd grasp of what is going on underneath the surface of the text:

- Write **'Malvolio's speech patterns here (Act V, Scene 1, lines 329–43) show his mind struggling between his sense of self-importance and the realisation that he has been thoroughly humiliated'.** This is better than **'The way Malvolio speaks makes him sound increasingly angry'.**
- You could identify some of the techniques Shakespeare uses to portray a character dramatically. For example:

> **When Malvolio interrupts the party in Act II Scene 3, he speaks like a typical Puritan –** 'Do ye make an ale-house of my lady's house ...?' **– in biblical rhythms so that Maria's verdict on him later on in the scene is justified –** 'The devil a Puritan that he is ... an affectioned ass, that cons state without book, and utters it by great swarths: the best persuaded of himself' **(lines 146–8).**

Or, 'to show how Olivia's love for Cesario is self-deluded and artificial, Shakespeare puts the dialogue into rhyming couplets at the end of Act III Scene 2'.

- Instead of using references/quotations to illustrate a particular kind of love in the play, you could use them to develop an idea about the delusory nature of the emotion and the language used to express it:

Feste's comment to Viola (Cesario) that 'A sentence is but a chev'ril glove to a good wit – how quickly the wrong side may be turned outward!' (I.2.11–13) reflects on the many unreliable statements – many about love – made in the play. Orsino rapidly transfers his affections to Viola as if everything he had said about his love for Olivia was forgotten. Olivia easily falls for Cesario shortly after claiming to turn her back upon the world. And, in the subplot, there are the meaningless words of the forged letter and Sir Andrew's challenge. 'Foolery', as Feste observes, does indeed 'walk about the orb like the sun, it shines everywhere' (III.1.39–40).

A candidate who is capable of arriving at unusual, well-supported judgements *independently* is likely to receive the highest marks.

CHECK YOUR ANSWER

Read through your answer carefully. It is generally an unpleasant experience – for all of us – but you will be amazed how many silly errors you can detect and put right before the paper disappears into the system.

If you find you have missed putting in paragraphs, do not rewrite the whole essay, simply put a line where the paragraph should end and write NP (new paragraph) in the margin.

Now take a break!

SAMPLE ESSAY PLAN

A typical essay question on *Twelfth Night* is followed by a sample essay plan in note form. This does not present the only answer to the question, merely one answer. Do not be afraid to include your own ideas and leave out some of the ones in this sample! Remember that quotations are essential to prove and illustrate the points you make.

Describe the different forms of disguise and deception that feature in *Twelfth Night*.

INTRODUCTION

This should clearly outline how you are going to deal with the question, briefly informing the reader how you will interpret the key terms, i.e. 'disguise' and 'deception':

- Viola's disguise as Cesario
- How disguise or deception contribute to the comedy
- How some characters are deceived about their true natures

VIOLA'S DISGUISE AS CESARIO

- Enables her to work for Orsino as a messenger
- Causes Olivia to fall in love with her
- Prevents Viola from expressing her love for Orsino
- Contributes to the dramatic ironies
- Causes the complications of mistaken identity

DISGUISE OR DECEPTION CONTRIBUTES TO MOST OF THE COMEDY

- The gulling of Malvolio
- Sir Andrew is encouraged to believe he has a chance with Olivia
- Sir Andrew and Cesario are tricked into a duel
- Feste dresses up as 'Sir Topas'
- Sir Andrew mistakes Sebastian for Cesario

EXAMINER'S SECRET

Avoid topics that have nothing directly to do with the question.

DID YOU KNOW?

Tudor and Stuart paintings at the National Portrait Gallery, London, will give you some idea of the Elizabethan love of display – beautiful clothes, richly ornamented, of which the Puritans so much disapproved.

SOME CHARACTERS ARE DECEIVED ABOUT THEIR TRUE NATURES

- Olivia adopts the pretence of mourning
- Orsino deludes himself that he loves Olivia
- The puritanical Malvolio is tricked into the role of Olivia's suitor and becomes a smiling 'courtier'

CONCLUSIONS

This will draw all the material you have used in the main body of the essay together, but should not just repeat everything you have written. If possible try to add an extra idea to give the reader something to think about, e.g. word-play is also a form of disguise and the numerous puns in the play reflect this theme on a linguistic level (see the conversation between Viola and Feste in Act III Scene 1).

FURTHER QUESTIONS

Make a plan as shown above and attempt these questions.

1. Describe the kind of love which is experienced by Orsino.
2. In what ways might we feel pity for Malvolio at the end of the play?
3. Show how Feste is connected to both the romantic and the comic plots.
4. Describe Viola's character as it is shown throughout the play.
5. How does the dramatic irony contribute to both the main plot and the subplot?
6. Compare the characters of Olivia and Viola.
7. Analyse the structure of *Twelfth Night*. How does Shakespeare keep the audience interested in the story and its characters?
8. Why is Malvolio excluded from the general happiness at the end of the play? Trace his role in the play.
9. Analyse some examples of contrasting speech styles in the play.
10. Write a character study of Sir Toby Belch.

CHECK THE BOOK

The Terrible Tudors by Terry Deary and Neil Tongue (1993) provides an entertaining, informative and accessible history book on the period.

Literary terms

alliteration a sequence of repeated sounds in a stretch of language

antitheses words balanced in contrast

blank verse unrhymed iambic pentameter: a line of five iambs

caesura a pause within a line of verse, caused by the natural organisation of the language into phrases, clauses and sentences

carpe diem (Latin for 'seize the day') this denotes a theme or subject common in literature: the plea or invitation to enjoy youth and life quickly, before the onset of dull maturity or death. This is often combined with an offer of love

Commedia dell'arte a form of drama in sixteenth-century Italy in which travelling companies of actors improvised comic plays around standard plots using stock characters

conventions all forms of literature are best understood or enjoyed when the reader or audience is aware of certain common features of the particular kind of literature in question: these common features are the 'conventions' of that form

diction the choice of words in a work of literature

dramatic irony this occurs when the development of the plot allows the audience to possess more information about what is happening than some of the characters themselves have

end-stopped a line of verse in which the end of the line coincides with an essential grammatical pause

enjambement describes a line of poetry which is not **end-stopped** and which continues into the next line

genre the term for a kind or type of literature. The major genres of literature are poetry, drama and the novel (prose). These can be subdivided into further genres, such as lyric, narrative verse, comedy, tragedy, short story, autobiography, biography and so on

hyperbole a figure of speech reliant on exaggeration

iamb the commonest metrical foot in English verse, a weak stress followed by a strong stress, *ti-tum*

iambic pentameter a line of five iambic feet. The most common metrical pattern found in English verse

metaphor a metaphor is when two different things or ideas are fused together: one thing is described as being another thing e.g. 'when the rich golden shaft / Hath kill'd the flock of all affections' (I.1.35–6)

metre the pattern of stressed and unstressed syllables in a line of verse

oxymoron a figure of speech in which contrasting terms are brought together: 'The Fortunate Unhappy' (II.5.159)

paradoxes something said which is absurd – a self-contradictory statement

pathos moments in works of art which invoke strong feelings of pity and sorrow are said to have this quality

poetic verse a style of speech in Shakespeare's plays using rhyming couplets and a strong rhythmic pulse to the line

prose any language that is not patterned by the regularity of some kind of metre

pun a play on words: two widely different meanings are drawn out of a single word, usually for comic purposes

rhyming couplet a pair of rhymed lines, of any metre e.g. 'O time, thou must untangle this, not I, / It is too hard a knot for me t'untie' (II.2.139–40)

LITERARY TERMS

romantic comedy an Elizabethan style of comedy concerning love, difficulties often involving mistaken identities, an escape from the real world into a quasi-magical setting, and a happy ending (see also *As You Like It*)

simile a figure of speech in which one thing is said to be like another, always containing the word 'like' or 'as'

soliloquy a dramatic convention which allows a character in a play to speak directly to the audience – as if thinking aloud about motives, feelings and decisions

stock characters/situations all genres make use of recurrent elements of plot, characterisation and situations which may become a defining aspect of that genre, part of its conventions. See Commedia dell'arte and conventions

subplot a subsidiary action running parallel with the main plot of a play or novel

verse paragraph division of blank verse into large, irregular units

wit originally meaning 'sense', 'understanding' or 'intelligence', the word came to refer to the kind of poetic intelligence which combines or contrasts ideas and expressions in an unexpected and intellectually pleasing way

CHECKPOINT HINTS/ANSWERS

CHECKPOINT 1 The *Comedy of Errors* by Shakespeare also features twins.

CHECKPOINT 2 Orsino is in a kind of dream. He seems to be someone who has based a great fantasy of love upon one single meeting with Olivia.

CHECKPOINT 3 A rapport which can be established with the audience through its knowledge of the disguise. Olivia and Viola have points of similarity to make Orsino's transference of affection to the latter more believable.

CHECKPOINT 4 Sir Toby is an embarrassment to Olivia (see Maria I.3.5–6) for his 'quaffing and drinking'. Maria's frank attitude to him shows she is a match for his difficult character. Sir Toby flatters Sir Andrew to manipulate him.

CHECKPOINT 5 Think about Olivia's pleasure in the fool's wit and her judgement on Malvolio. This tells us about her intelligence and liberality. Her curiosity about Cesario is girlish – she is still interested in men despite her mourning.

CHECKPOINT 6 At the end of the scene Malvolio goes after Cesario. Olivia is hooked and audience expectations raised: 'Fate, slow thy force ... What is decreed, must be' (lines 314–15).

CHECKPOINT 7 Sebastian is more emotional and impulsive, as we will see later on in the play, and is sure Viola has drowned.

CHECKPOINT 8 The last lines of the last three scenes all point to future events: the audience will be anticipating the future appearance of Sebastian and the resolution of the story-lines.

CHECKPOINT 9 Malvolio's biblical address and rhythm (he is a Puritan). He uses pretentious vocabulary – '...any mitigation or remorse of voice' (lines 91–2). He looks down on the revellers and compares them to common people who drink in ale-houses – 'coziers' (tinkers). When he talks about Olivia his tone and the words he uses take on a pompous quality – 'she's nothing allied to your disorders' (line 97).

CHECKPOINT 10 He is a Puritan, a time-pleaser, affected, pretentious and conceited.

CHECKPOINT 11 Orsino sees himself as the constant lover. The audience, already knowing Viola loves him, might expect his 'changeable' mind to turn.

CHECKPOINT 12 Shakespeare makes Viola express her feelings in a fiction about her father's daughter.

CHECKPOINT 13 The two dialogues between Orsino and Cesario are separated by Feste's song, the theme of which is unrequited love and which reflects the emotional situation of both Orsino and Viola.

CHECKPOINT 14 Malvolio's ludicrous ambitions and pretension are at their height. This is a great comic moment in the play and should be visualised. Try mapping out the scene for a stage production.

CHECKPOINT 15 The scenes of the main romantic plot alternate with those of the **subplot**. By starting this scene with some of the comic characters, Shakespeare begins to bring the two plots together.

CHECKPOINT 16 So that the disguise can remain undetected.

CHECKPOINT 17 We learn more of Sir Andrew's stupidity from the fact that he continues to believe he has a chance with Olivia and allows himself to be duped by Fabian and Sir Toby, the latter still interested in his money.

CHECKPOINT 18 Sir Andrew is foolish, but Malvolio is arrogant to believe that Olivia can love him.

CHECKPOINT 19 The references are lines 25–6 'an icicle on a dutchman's beard' and lines 76–7 'the new map with the augmentation of the Indies'

CHECKPOINT HINTS/ANSWERS

CHECKPOINT 20 When Antonio mistakes Cesario for Sebastian dramatic tension is heightened by his resentment.

CHECKPOINT 21 Olivia is expecting Cesario but it is Malvolio who comes to woo her. Sir Andrew comes with his challenge for further gulling. Sir Toby and Fabian wind up Cesario. Then, at the climax, Antonio is arrested after he tries to protect Cesario (whom he believes is Sebastian).

CHECKPOINT 22 Sir Toby stops the 'knavery' (IV.2.69–73) and stops Feste teasing Malvolio.

CHECKPOINT 23 It's a dark scene in more ways than one because Malvolio could very well be insane. This could make us more sympathetic to him. Madness was not treated with any compassion.

CHECKPOINT 24 Consider the light, the bars, the space of the enclosure, the levels of the stage.

CHECKPOINT 25 Sebastian appears as a strong man at the start and meets Olivia for the first time – her 'true' love. At the end of the Act he appears again and marries her. He is in a dream, he thinks.

CHECKPOINT 26 All the strands start to come together, from the interception of Malvolio's letter to the appearance of Sebastian.

CHECKPOINT 27 Antonio accuses Cesario of betraying him. Then Olivia, also believing Cesario is Sebastian, accuses him of betraying their marriage vows. And Orsino accuses Cesario of alienating his love for Olivia.

CHECKPOINT 28 For example, Orsino recognises Antonio. Orsino recognises Olivia's love for 'Cesario'. Viola recognises Sebastian.

CHECKPOINT 29 He is angry, bewildered, resentful and finally vengeful.

CHECKPOINT 30 A recognition scene between twins or disguised lovers was a convention of comedy: Viola must gradually come to recognise her lost brother, just as Sebastian himself must come to recognise his lost sister through her disguise as 'Cesario'.

Test answers

Test yourself (Act I)

1 Orsino *(Scene 1)*

2 Valentine *(Scene 1)*

3 Captain *(Scene 2)*

4 Viola *(Scene 2)*

5 Sir Toby Belch *(Scene 3)*

6 Sir Andrew Aguecheek *(Scene 3)*

7 Malvolio *(Scene 5)*

8 Orsino *(Scene 5)*

Test yourself (Act II)

1 Sebastian *(Scene 1)*

2 Viola *(Scene 2)*

3 Sir Toby Belch *(Scene 3)*

4 Maria *(Scene 3)*

5 Sir Andrew Aguecheek *(Scene 3)*

6 Malvolio *(Scene 3)*

7 Malvolio *(Scene 3)*

8 Orsino *(Scene 4)*

Test yourself (Act III)

1 Feste *(Scene 1)*

2 Viola *(Scene 1)*

3 Maria *(Scene 2)*

4 Antonio *(Scene 3)*

5 Malvolio *(Scene 4)*

6 Sir Andrew Aguecheek *(Scene 4)*

7 Cesario *(Scene 4)*

8 Sebastian (Cesario) *(Scene 4)*

Test yourself (Act IV)

1 Feste *(Scene 1)*

2 Sebastian *(Scene 1)*

3 Feste ('Sir Topas') *(Scene 2)*

4 Sir Toby Belch *(Scene 2)*

5 Malvolio *(Scene 2)*

6 Sebastian *(Scene 3)*

7 Sebastian *(Scene 3)*

8 Sebastian *(Scene 1)*

9 Sebastian *(Scene 1)*

10 Malvolio *(Scene 2)*

Test yourself (Act V)

1 Olivia *(Scene 1)*

2 Cesario *(Scene 1)*

3 Sebastian *(Scene 1)*

4 Malvolio *(Scene 1)*

5 Sebastian *(Scene 1)*

6 Cesario *(Scene 1)*

7 Olivia *(Scene 1)*

8 Olivia *(Scene 1)*

9 Malvolio *(Scene 1)*

Notes

NOTES

York Notes for GCSE

Maya Angelou
I Know Why the Caged Bird Sings
Jane Austen
Pride and Prejudice
Alan Ayckbourn
Absent Friends
Elizabeth Barrett Browning
Selected Poems
Robert Bolt
A Man for All Seasons
Harold Brighouse
Hobson's Choice
Charlotte Brontë
Jane Eyre
Emily Brontë
Wuthering Heights
Shelagh Delaney
A Taste of Honey
Charles Dickens
David Copperfield
Great Expectations
Hard Times
Oliver Twist
Roddy Doyle
Paddy Clarke Ha Ha Ha
George Eliot
Silas Marner
The Mill on the Floss
Anne Frank
The Diary of a Young Girl
William Golding
Lord of the Flies
Oliver Goldsmith
She Stoops to Conquer
Willis Hall
The Long and the Short and the Tall
Thomas Hardy
Far from the Madding Crowd
The Mayor of Casterbridge
Tess of the d'Urbervilles
The Withered Arm and other Wessex Tales
L.P. Hartley
The Go-Between
Seamus Heaney
Selected Poems
Susan Hill
I'm the King of the Castle
Barry Hines
A Kestrel for a Knave
Louise Lawrence
Children of the Dust
Harper Lee
To Kill a Mockingbird
Laurie Lee
Cider with Rosie
Arthur Miller
The Crucible
A View from the Bridge
Robert O'Brien
Z for Zachariah
Frank O'Connor
My Oedipus Complex and Other Stories
George Orwell
Animal Farm
J.B. Priestley
An Inspector Calls
When We Are Married
Willy Russell
Educating Rita
Our Day Out
J.D. Salinger
The Catcher in the Rye
William Shakespeare
Henry IV Part 1
Henry V
Julius Caesar
Macbeth
The Merchant of Venice
A Midsummer Night's Dream
Much Ado About Nothing
Romeo and Juliet
The Tempest
Twelfth Night
George Bernard Shaw
Pygmalion
Mary Shelley
Frankenstein
R.C. Sherriff
Journey's End
Rukshana Smith
Salt on the snow
John Steinbeck
Of Mice and Men
Robert Louis Stevenson
Dr Jekyll and Mr Hyde
Jonathan Swift
Gulliver's Travels
Robert Swindells
Daz 4 Zoe
Mildred D. Taylor
Roll of Thunder, Hear My Cry
Mark Twain
Huckleberry Finn
James Watson
Talking in Whispers
Edith Wharton
Ethan Frome
William Wordsworth
Selected Poems
A Choice of Poets
Mystery Stories of the Nineteenth Century including The Signalman
Nineteenth Century Short Stories
Poetry of the First World War
Six Women Poets

York Notes advanced

Margaret Atwood
Cat's Eye
The Handmaid's Tale

Jane Austen
Emma
Mansfield Park
Persuasion
Pride and Prejudice
Sense and Sensibility

Alan Bennett
Talking Heads

William Blake
Songs of Innocence and of Experience

Charlotte Brontë
Jane Eyre
Villette

Emily Brontë
Wuthering Heights

Angela Carter
Nights at the Circus

Geoffrey Chaucer
The Franklin's Prologue and Tale
The Miller's Prologue and Tale
The Prologue to the Canterbury Tales
The Wife of Bath's Prologue and Tale

Samuel Coleridge
Selected Poems

Joseph Conrad
Heart of Darkness

Daniel Defoe
Moll Flanders

Charles Dickens
Bleak House
Great Expectations
Hard Times

Emily Dickinson
Selected Poems

John Donne
Selected Poems

Carol Ann Duffy
Selected Poems

George Eliot
Middlemarch
The Mill on the Floss

T.S. Eliot
Selected Poems
The Waste Land

F. Scott Fitzgerald
The Great Gatsby

E.M. Forster
A Passage to India

Brian Friel
Translations

Thomas Hardy
Jude the Obscure
The Mayor of Casterbridge
The Return of the Native
Selected Poems
Tess of the d'Urbervilles

Seamus Heaney
Selected Poems from 'Opened Ground'

Nathaniel Hawthorne
The Scarlet Letter

Homer
The Iliad
The Odyssey

Aldous Huxley
Brave New World

Kazuo Ishiguro
The Remains of the Day

Ben Jonson
The Alchemist

James Joyce
Dubliners

John Keats
Selected Poems

Christopher Marlowe
Doctor Faustus
Edward II

Arthur Miller
Death of a Salesman

John Milton
Paradise Lost Books I & II

Toni Morrison
Beloved

George Orwell
Nineteen Eighty-Four

Sylvia Plath
Selected Poems

Alexander Pope
Rape of the Lock & Selected Poems

William Shakespeare
Antony and Cleopatra
As You Like It
Hamlet
Henry IV Part I
King Lear
Macbeth
Measure for Measure
The Merchant of Venice
A Midsummer Night's Dream
Much Ado About Nothing
Othello
Richard II
Richard III
Romeo and Juliet
The Taming of the Shrew
The Tempest
Twelfth Night
The Winter's Tale

George Bernard Shaw
Saint Joan

Mary Shelley
Frankenstein

Jonathan Swift
Gulliver's Travels and A Modest Proposal

Alfred Tennyson
Selected Poems

Virgil
The Aeneid

Alice Walker
The Color Purple

Oscar Wilde
The Importance of Being Earnest

Tennessee Williams
A Streetcar Named Desire

Jeanette Winterson
Oranges Are Not the Only Fruit

John Webster
The Duchess of Malfi

Virginia Woolf
To the Lighthouse

W.B. Yeats
Selected Poems

Metaphysical Poets